ESCAPE FROM SELFHOOD

PSYCHOANALYTIC IDEAS AND APPLICATIONS SERIES

ESCAPE FROM SELFHOOD
Breaking Boundaries
and Craving for Oneness

Ilany Kogan

Foreword by
Andrea Celenza

Psychoanalytic Ideas and Applications Series

**International
Psychoanalytical
Association**

LONDON

First published in 2007 by

The International Psychoanalytical Association
Broomhills
Woodside Lane
London N12 8UD
United Kingdom

British Library Cataloguing in Publication Data

A C.I.P. for this book is available from the British Library

ISBN: 978-1-905888-05-4

10 9 8 7 6 5 4 3 2 1

Produced for the IPA by Communication Crafts

Printed in Great Britain

www.ipa.org.uk

In memory of my dear friend
Janine Chasseguet-Smirgel

CONTENTS

PSYCHOANALYTIC IDEAS AND APPLICATIONS SERIES

IPA Publications Committee

The Publications Committee of the International Psychoanalytical Association continues, with this volume, the series: "Psychoanalytic Ideas and Applications".

The aim is to focus on the scientific production of significant authors whose works are outstanding contributions to the development of the psychoanalytic field and to set out relevant ideas and themes, generated during the history of psychoanalysis, that deserve to be discussed by present psychoanalysts.

The relationship between psychoanalytic ideas and their applications has to be put forward from the perspective of theory, clinical practice, technique, and research so as to maintain their validity for contemporary psychoanalysis.

The Publication Committee's objective is to share these ideas with the psychoanalytic community and with professionals in other related disciplines, in order to expand their knowledge and generate a productive interchange between the text and the reader.

We are grateful to Ilany Kogan for having accepted our proposal to develop her work into this book with enthusiasm and with generosity. Particular thanks are also due to Salman Akhtar, who has steered this project from the time of the previous Committee to enable us to publish it.

Leticia Glocer Fiorini
Chair, IPA Publications Committee

ACKNOWLEDGEMENTS

Writing a book is always an experience that involves the other, even when it is written by one person. In addition to the unknown audience, it includes the help and support of others.

First I wish to thank my friend Salman Akhtar for his invaluable help. His astute critical comments, as well as his appreciation and encouragement, enabled me to bring this book to completion.

The book includes a detailed description of an analysis, a process that was fuelled by numerous discussions with friends and colleagues. I am grateful to Alice Buras, Anna Gertler, Dahlia Lapidot, Cila Smolarsky, and Gisele Vered for their fruitful input, especially in moments of impasse in therapy.

I also want to thank Ms. Chava Cassel, my English editor, for her dedication and support in difficult moments of the creative process, and Eric and Klara King, of Communication Crafts, for their efforts in the realization of this project.

Finally, I am grateful to my patient, who allowed me to accompany him on his painful analytic journey. The work of the analytic couple, as a shared experience, forms the substance of this book.

ABOUT THE AUTHOR

Ilany Kogan is a Training Analyst at the Israel Psychoanalytic Society; a Member of the Scientific Advisory Board of the Fritz-Bauer Institut for Holocaust studies, Frankfurt, Germany; Clinical Supervisor at the Department of Children and Adolescents, Eppendorf University Hospital, Hamburg, Germany, and of MAP candidates, Munich, Germany; Supervisor of the Psychotherapy Centre for the Child and Adolescent, Bucharest, Romania; and a teacher and supervisor at the IPA psychoanalytic group, Istanbul, Turkey. For many years she worked extensively with Holocaust survivors' offspring and published and presented many papers on the topic. She is author of *The Cry of Mute Children: A Psychoanalytic Perspective of the Second Generation of the Holocaust* (London & New York: Free Association Books, 1995; German edition, Frankfurt: Fischer Verlag, 1998; Romanian edition, Bucharest: Editura Trei, 2001; French edition, Geneva & Paris: Delachaux et Niestlé, 2001; Croatian edition, Zagreb: antiBarbarus, 2005). She was awarded the Elise M. Hayman Award for the Study of the Holocaust and Genocide at the IPA Congress, Rio de Janeiro (2005), for her work in the realm of the second generation of the Holocaust.

FOREWORD

Andrea Celenza

The creation of boundaries is at once a psychic necessity and an illusion. The need to draw lines allows for the existence of categories—this is this and not that—and, in this way, boundaries make thinking possible. We also establish rules that demarcate psychic space: don't touch me there, don't ask me that. However, there are no real lines, even on a physical level, just *horizons* where one entity meets another and the outer skin defines the borders between the two. In the psychic world, the lines are more blurry still. Who is to say where one's self ends and the other begins?

The boundary demarcating two separate existences is a needed perceptual differentiation in order that our thoughts and feelings may be categorized and felt as me-not-you. Thus, it is through boundaries that the self is born. Yet, in relationships, as in analysis,

Andrea Celenza, PhD, is an Assistant Clinical Professor at Harvard Medical School and is on the faculty of two psychoanalytic institutes: Boston Psychoanalytic Society and Institute and Massachusetts Institute for Psychoanalysis. She is the primary consultant to the Northeast Episcopal Diocese on issues of sexual misconduct in the clergy and a member of the Committee on Psychoanalytic Education of the American Psychoanalytic Association.

these psychic boundaries are invisible, and the distinction of one's self as different and separate from another must be asserted and reasserted in a continuous and ongoing way.

Lines both clarify our own wishes and make plain their impossibility. The desire to fuse with mother in blissful cocoon-like oneness inevitably includes her destruction. If we embrace our loving self and strive to embody only these (libidinal) urges, we leave a murderer on the loose. In the same way, it is a profound realization that we can both infinitely love and intensely hate the same person. Since psychoanalysis aims to help our patients to experience the full spectrum of feeling, destructive wishes will inevitably emerge in the treatment dyad despite the wish to keep them underground.

Through her analysis of her patient, "David", Ilany Kogan shows us how to reckon with several existential questions. How to keep separate the need for soothing and the wish to destroy? How to escape from a destructive past that has taken over the needed present mother yet still make contact with her? How to hold onto the soothing mother and escape from her strangulating grip? How to fuse with mother in a oneness cocoon and yet not destroy her psychic separateness? These are all questions that the author takes up, and through the treatment she comes to terms with the ways in which David lives them out. In one instance, David related how a woman had said to him, "Calm your father, calm him", but what the author thought she heard David say was "Kill your father, kill him"—a prescient mishearing that symbolizes the challenge of the analysis itself.

Establishing boundaries requires access to one's aggression—the ability to say "No, I don't want that" is essentially stating: "This is not me." Yet how does one come to terms with such aggressive strivings if there is a fear that one's anger is murderous? Traumatized individuals often cope with the residue of anger, an inevitable consequence of trauma, by disavowing its existence. Then the assertion of limits becomes an impossibility, since to access anger is to access a murderer. As the author shows us, the analyst must demonstrate to the patient that his anger can be survived (Winnicott, 1971).

There is a universal wish stemming from childhood but persisting throughout life that entails a return to the womb, a safe retreat where wishes and needs are met without recompense or expectation. Such is the nature of oneness fantasies that have their origin in infancy, probably the only time that such fantasies are actually fulfilled.

Oneness fantasies are also stirred up by the treatment itself, partly deriving from the structure of the analytic setup: for fifty minutes the patient really is the "one and only", if for just this brief time. Thus, the asymmetric distribution of attention fulfils lifelong wishes—to have the mother's gaze fixed solely upon the self and to return to the soothing cocoon of the womb. Only in the womb are one's wishes intuited and gratified without the need for the jarring sound of words. It is only with birth and the tragic reality of separateness that language becomes a necessity.

The desire to return to the womb/cocoon that exists in all of us can become a defensive structure beckoning an illusory retreat protected from the traumas of the outside and inside world. How do Holocaust survivors (of any number of generations removed) rein-vest themselves in life, in hope and optimism? From where does the desire and capacity to live outside the oneness cocoon derive? Ilany Kogan invites us to peer inside her patient's inner world and into their treatment relationship to see where such a wellspring of new birth might exist. She demonstrates how the groundwork is laid so that David can allow both himself and his analyst to see and experi-ence his destructive potential. By allowing his aggressive fantasies to emerge and having the courage to face and place into perspective its origins, these essential urges transform into a strength and verve for living that he can now access, control, and use.

Separateness is a profound and frightening achievement requir-ing the relinquishing of treasured fantasies. To face the reality that there is no hiding place, no safe cocoon or psychic retreat (Steiner, 1993), no universe without obstacles (Chasseguet-Smirgel, 1978), and no way to erase the past is a profound giving up. For traumatized individuals, such mourning also requires an acceptance of human destructive potential—one's own as well as the capacity for our dear-est love objects to betray and abandon. The longing for oneness be-comes a psychic retreat where the dissolution of the self symbolizes the dissolution of murderous aggression.

This book is a scholarly weave of various writings on psychic boundaries—Akhtar (2006), Chasseguet-Smirgel (1978), Gabbard and Lester (1995), Mahler, Pine, and Bergmann (1975), and Winni-cott (1971), to name a few. Through the use of a psychoanalytic exploration with David, the child of Holocaust survivors, the author takes us on an internal journey of attempted escape from boundedness. She bravely faced the destructive potential in her patient's fantasies and wishes by finding resonances within herself. Through her courageous self-explorations, she reassured her patient that feelings and wishes can be survived, outlining a pathway to renewed hope in a horrifying world. The patient finds his resolution and relinquishes his omnipotent defence—in, as the author so aptly phrases it, an "Escape from Selfhood".

ESCAPE FROM SELFHOOD

"It may be that one life is a punishment
For another, as the son's life for the father."

Wallace Stevens, "Esthétique du Mal"
(1954), lines 274–275

Introduction

The Holocaust was a cataclysmic event that changed the shape of human history forever. It was an unprecedented, systematic attempt to achieve "racial purity" through the extermination of innocent people. Although there is historical evidence of other tragedies involving genocide, only the Holocaust involved a master plan for the deliberate extinction of a group of people who were regarded as unfit to inhabit the earth with other mortals. Bergmann and Jucovy state:

> The concept adopted by the Nazis in devising the Final Solution was the fulfilment of an ideology of hate—an apocalyptic end in itself. Sophisticated technology was applied to the organized and relentless slaughter of a people—a slaughter on a scale surpassing any anti-Semitic crimes of the past. [Bergmann & Jucovy, 1982, p. 4]

During this period of infamy, the boundaries between the human and the inhuman were broken. Six million of Europe's Jews were murdered, and along with them a rich and thriving culture disappeared.

Those who survived the Holocaust suffered major immediate and long-term effects. These included post-traumatic stress disorder

(PTSD) and ongoing manifestations of annihilation anxiety such as distrust, a tendency to isolation, and numbing of feelings. Survivors often experienced intense depression that led to complete social withdrawal, seclusion, and profound apathy (Lifton, 1978). Many had difficulty "reinvesting" in life, and they were deeply ambivalent about founding new families (Krystal, 1968).

The Holocaust affected the lives not only of the survivors, but also of the second- and third-generation offspring of these victims throughout the world. Many researchers assume the inevitability of transmitting pathology from survivors to their children (Kestenberg, 1972; Trossman, 1968). They argue that since Holocaust experiences negatively affected the survivors' capacity for human relations, they are unable to be effective parents, which has damaging psychological ramifications for themselves and for their offspring. As Gampel (2005) metaphorically describes it, the traces that reside in the psyches and bodies of those who have been through the Holocaust have a "radioactive" effect on their offspring.

Undertaking a study of the impact of the Holocaust on the survivors' offspring poses an almost insuperable challenge. It might be considered presumptuous to attempt to objectively describe the unspeakable horror of the past and its colossal repercussions for the next generation. But it would be even more presumptuous not to take up this formidable challenge, if for no other reason than to attempt to alleviate some of the suffering that exists to this very day among second- and third-generation offspring of Holocaust survivors. The role that the Holocaust played in shaping the offspring's character formation and cognitive and emotional development has indeed been examined in depth in the psychoanalytic literature (for a review of the literature, see Kestenberg & Brenner, 1996; Volkan, Ast, & Greer, 2002).

On psychic boundaries

This book explores one of the extreme pathological conditions emanating from the complex relationship between Holocaust survivor parents and their offspring: the breaking of boundaries. To better understand this phenomenon, we must first examine the concept of psychic boundaries.

The question of what is meant by, and also what constitutes, an intrapsychic boundary is a highly abstract and elusive one. Yet the concept of boundary is without question a central and pivotal one in psychoanalysis and is frequently referred to and employed at the levels of both clinical discussion and metapsychological explanation. Similar to other psychoanalytic terms, though, it is difficult to give to this concept a clear and uncontroversial definition (Sandler, 1983).

In his extensive review of boundaries, Erlich (1990) claims that this concept has been used in reference to numerous and highly varied phenomena, ranging from schizophrenia through altered ego states, primary-process thinking, dreams, and borderline conditions and reaching all the way to aspects of maturity/immaturity, levels of endurance of stress and frustration, achievements in the area of separation–individuation, and levels of differentiation in the definition of self and identity. The centrality and impressive elasticity of the boundary concept are thus reflected in its serving as a useful and meaningful dimension in the areas of development, psychodynamics, and psychopathology.

I shall first present a brief review of this concept and then examine some of the elements that influence the formation of boundaries from the beginning of life through adolescence and maturity.

From Freud's (1930a) early work on "oceanic feelings" to current research in this area (Gabbard & Lester, 1995), the concept of psychic boundaries has been the subject of much theorizing. In *Civilization and Its Discontents*, Freud dealt briefly with the concept of boundaries:

> Pathology has made us acquainted with a great number of states in which the boundary lines between the ego and the external world are uncertain or in which they are actually drawn incorrectly. There are cases in which parts of a person's own body, even portions of his own mental life—his perceptions, thoughts and feelings—, appear alien to him and not belonging to his ego. . . . Thus even the feeling of our own ego is subject to disturbances and the boundaries of the ego are not constant. [1930a, p. 66]

Federn (1952), a prominent ego psychologist, conceptualized boundaries as a function and attribute of the ego. The ego boundary is a peripheral sense organ that discriminates between what is real and what is unreal. Encompassing mental as well as physical dimensions, the ego boundary incorporates both inner and outer boundaries. Unlike Freud, who was interested in the dream and its relation to the psychic life of the individual, Federn focused his attention on transitional states—that is, the transition between sleep and waking, between waking and sleep, and "more generally, between different levels of vigilance in the ego" (Anzieu, 1989, p. 88). For Federn, inner ego boundaries, separating the ego from the id and from the superego, constituted a type of barrier against unconscious drives and fantasies; external boundaries helped to separate the ego from the external world. These boundaries fluctuate continuously.

Following Federn's work, for a number of years the distinction between inner and outer boundaries received little or no theoretical attention. Then, object-relations theorists such as Jacobson (1964) introduced the concept of boundaries as the demarcation between self- and object-representations by which an individual establishes a separateness between experience of the self and the simultaneous experience of the object. Jacobson focused on interpersonal outer boundaries and their internalized dimensions. She maintained that, during development, self- and object-representations undergo repeated fusions and separations, but a normal outcome "presupposes the constitution of well defined self representations separated by distinct, firm boundaries from the likewise realistic representations of the love object" (Jacobson, 1964, pp. 51–52).

Continuing Federn's line of thinking, Anzieu (1989) proposed the concept of the "skin ego", a complex theoretical construct that is primarily a psychological body envelope. This concept includes an early and fundamental element in the formation of the ego, built on the proprioception and symbolization of the skin. The envelope functions as a permeable psychic boundary separating self from object. The skin is a container, an instrument of separation, and a divisionary line that the mental apparatus, treating it as a psychophysiological given, draws upon, utilizes, and weaves into the evolving schemas of the differentiating self.

Landis (1970) further developed Federn's concept of boundaries, contending that boundaries differentiate the self both from aspects of the personality not represented in the conscious and from the world of external reality as it is psychologically experienced by the individual. In his experimental research, Landis dealt primarily with outer interpersonal boundaries. He measured permeability (looseness) and impermeability (firmness) of boundaries, which he regarded as internal functions of the ego. He believed that the range of pathological states (from schizophrenia to neurotic) was a function of the looseness or firmness of these boundaries.

Hartmann, in his book *Boundaries in the Mind* (1991), maintained that boundaries exist "in the mind". He reintroduced Federn's separation of inner and outer external boundaries, extending both categories. Lester, in her review of Hartmann's book, refers to his over-inclusive definition of boundaries:

> Whatever two entities in our mind or our worlds we are talking about, they can be conceptualized as relatively separate (having a thick boundary between them), or in communication (with a thin boundary between them)" [Lester, 1994, p. 411]

According to Hartmann, this dimension of the personality is best understood within the juxtaposition of these two opposite states. He put forward the hypothesis that thinness or thickness of boundaries relates both to constitutional factors and to early experiences such as trauma, deprivation, and a chaotic early life. In his view, early experience of a traumatic nature may predispose—although not predictably so—to the development of thin boundaries. Developmentally, infancy and early childhood are characterized by thin boundaries; in latency (ages 5 to 10 years), a solidifying and thickening of boundaries takes place. The degree of this thickening, according to Hartmann, depends on both genetic and environmental factors. He contended that the boundaries existing "in the mind" are a measurable dimension of the personality. A consistent finding among experimental subjects was that relatively thick boundaries correlate significantly with a strong identification with the same-sex parent. In his view, such identification contributes to the relative thickening of boundaries that parallels the cohesiveness of self-identity.

Hartmann also examined the importance of boundary structure in artistic creativity and the relationship of such structure to schizophrenia and other types of mental illness. He concluded that there is no simple correlation between these structures and creativity, although a certain openness, sensitivity, and fluidity (thinness of boundaries) are essential, but not sufficient, to artistic production. With reference to mental dysfunction, borderline and schizotypal personality disorders, as well as schizophrenia, are positively correlated with thin inner boundaries, while strongly thick inner boundaries are often identified in obsessive-compulsive personality structures. What is of theoretical interest is the finding that "there was far more psychopathology in those with 'thin inside, thick outside' pattern than in those who scored thin overall or thick overall" (1991, p. 200).

In this book, I wish to add the dimension of time to the concept of boundaries. It is the clear differentiation between past and present that enables us to be connected to our past without becoming prisoners of it. Among offspring of Holocaust survivors there is often no clear differentiation between past and present. For them, temporal boundaries may become permeable to the point that the past intrudes into the present and becomes the present. This is different from the phenomenon of "continuity amidst change" (Erikson, 1956), which is a hallmark of a healthy identity.

I now explore some elements of boundary formation and the establishment of a sense of separateness of the self from the beginning of life through the further stages of development. At the beginning of life, the sense of self is consolidated through sensations that stem from the physiological feedback accompanying bodily activities and the functioning of the senses. This issue has been explored in the psychoanalytic literature, as I now briefly review.

Freud (1923e) established the link between body and self by defining the ego as "first and foremost a bodily ego, not merely a surface, but itself a projection of a surface" (p. 26). By this, Freud underlined one of the most important factors that form the basis of identity.

Hoffer (1950) claimed that the distinction between self and not-self stems from the way one experiences one's body and what subsequently becomes environment; this is based on two sensations of the same quality elicited by the hand of the infant touching his or her own body. This factor contributes to the process of structural differentiation.

Mahler, Pine, and Bergmann (1975) stressed the growth of the ego as, first, functioning in the matrix of the narcissistic relationship and, later, in the object-relationship to the mother. When the child's capacity to use the mother as "a beacon of orientation in the world of reality" (Mahler, 1968) is deficient, the ego apparatus—which usually grows in the matrix of the ordinary devoted-mothering relationship (Winnicott, 1962)—fails to thrive; or, in Glover's terms (1956), the ego nuclei do not integrate, but fall apart.

Bick (1968) shed light on this idea from another angle. In her opinion, the body's skin functions as a boundary that has an internal meaning: it holds together the different parts of the personality, which, in their most primitive form, do not appear to possess a force that binds them together. This internal function of containing the parts of the self is dependent, initially, on the introjection of an external object that is experienced as capable of fulfilling this function. Children who have no opportunity of identifying with a containing object suffer from defective self-integration and from impaired differentiation between internal and external spaces.

Anzieu (1985), as well as Houzel (1987), elaborated upon Freud's idea of the ego as a structure charged with a precise psychic function—that is, to contain psychic excitation and block the free flow of quantities of excitation inside the mind (Freud, 1950 [1895]). The ego is the surface that draws the line of demarcation between the individual's internal and external worlds, between the internal psychic world and the psychic world of other people, a surface that Anzieu and Houzel refer to as a "psychic envelope".

Pines (1980) also stressed the fundamental importance of the skin for the development of the self. Pines viewed the skin as a means of communication between mother and infant, with the mother providing the holding environment. This is how primary identification of the self is established.

Other dimensions that influence the formation of boundaries particularly in adolescence were examined in depth by Erlich (1990). These dimensions are: cognitive processes, the impact of the superego, and relations with the object or the other. According to Ehrlic, cognitive processes have a great influence on the development of the sense of separateness of self and object. Basing himself on Jacobson (1964), who defined boundaries as a function of the level of differentiation of internal representations, he claims that these processes derive from the integration and sharpening of the intrapsychic representations of self and object. This implies a process of psychic development in the course of which mental representations become gradually more consolidated and increasingly well-differentiated.

Adolescence, in his view, is a period of development, in which the tremendous changes and upheavals undergone by the boundaries of self and ego are an outcome of the cognitive development that occurs at this stage. The cognitive development is expressed through transforming concrete operations into formal operations (Inhelder & Piaget, 1958). This observation does not contradict Anna Freud's

(1958, 1969) formulation that adolescent developmental disturbance originates in the encounter between increasing drives and a temporarily weakened ego. The temporary weakening of the ego is due to the increase in drives, as well as to the difficult passage to a new level of emotional and cognitive functioning.

Another dimension examined by Erlich (1990) is the impact of the superego on the formation of boundaries. The superego contributes to the establishment of boundaries from an entirely different direction—from the introjection of punitive and loving parental images and the identification with such representations in the course of its formation. The boundaries that are formed are around what may be referred to as "right and wrong", and they are connected to the introjected limitations especially concerning instinctual wishes. Such issues are associated with generation and class and with the allocation of power and authority as perceived and experienced by the oedipal and pre-oedipal child.

Object-relationships (what actually takes place between persons, particularly between people who are meaningfully and significantly related to each other) constitute a more mature level at which we encounter the issue of boundaries. This level encompasses separation–individuation processes and also includes relations between representations of self and object, as well as the drive investments and transformations these representations receive and undergo.

Hindered boundary formation

The normal boundaries existing between parents and children facilitate separation and individuation. The situation is different in the relationship with traumatized parents. However, before proceeding any further, a few words about trauma are in order. The term "trauma" was borrowed from the Greek, where it refers to a piercing of the skin, a breaking of the bodily envelope. Freud (1920g, 1926d [1925]) used the word metaphorically to emphasize how the mind too can be pierced and wounded by events, giving graphic force to his description of the mind being enveloped by a kind of skin or protective shield. Freud regarded trauma as an excess of external stimuli that overcomes the protective barriers against overstimulation, radically threatening the integrity of the personality. This may lead to long-lasting disturbances in ego functioning. The attack on ego boundaries can come from within just as from without.

Exploring the impact of trauma on boundaries from the developmental perspective, Salman Akhtar (1998) asserted that traumatized individuals may hinder the development of adequate boundaries in their children. This, in his opinion, is a universal phenomenon that may be the outcome of five different ways of relating to the child, which often operate in unison:

1. *Over-identifying with the child.* Traumatized parents may over-identify with the inherent fragility of their child and, as a result, are anxious about frustrating the child. Consequently, the child fails to develop an adequate distinction between realistic and wishful states of the self (and their respective relatedness with objects).

2. *Confusing ordinary parental control with cruelty.* Traumatized parents, being chronically (even if unconsciously) enraged, may be vulnerable to confusing their legitimate and needed assertion of parental control with destructive aggression. Ordinary parental control becomes, in their minds, akin to cruelty. This renders them unable to set limits for their child, who, as a result, is saddled with unbridled greed and omnipotence.

3. *Difficulty in excluding the child from any activity or sphere of life.* Traumatized parents frequently experience agonizing marginalization and "catastrophic aloneness" (Grand, 2000). In a naïve attempt to reverse this trauma, they often include their child in all spheres of their lives. Establishing generational boundaries is difficult for them; the primal scene either goes blank or becomes a public scene. In either case, the child becomes oedipally triumphant and cocky. The parental marriage in cases of traumatized parents may sometimes be inappropriate (e.g., with marked sociocultural or age differences between partners), a fact that also facilitates this tendency on the offspring's part.

4. *Spoiling the child due to envy.* Traumatized parents may envy their offspring for their more fortunate realities. This envy might cause them to damage their child's normal emotional growth. The spoiling effort may be a reaction formation to the parents' own hostility or destructivity towards the child. Either way, healthy boundary creation is precluded.

5. *Re-enacting one's own traumas.* Traumatized parents tend to identify with their aggressors and may enact scenarios of sadistic
destruction of boundaries with their offspring. Under the sway
of instinctually driven repetition compulsion, they relive, again
and again, the tormented moments when their own "protective
shield" (Freud, 1950 [1895]) was broken—only this time, they
may enact the role of perpetrator.

Permeability of boundaries
in Holocaust survivor parents and their offspring

Hindered boundary formation is a universal phenomenon among
traumatized parents and their offspring. In this book I focus on a
specific traumatized group—Holocaust survivor parents—and the
impact of their very particular type of traumatization on their offspring. There exists a cluster of damaged boundaries between Holocaust survivor parents and their children, in addition to the more
universal phenomenon of hindered boundary formation. This cluster
includes the permeability and blurring of temporal boundaries between past and present, between self and object, and between fantasy
and reality (Auerhahn & Prelinger, 1983; Gampel, 1982, 2005; Kestenberg, 1980; Kogan, 1995, 2003). The permeability of boundaries
in these three realms leads to "primitive identification" (Freyberg,
1980; Grubrich-Simitis, 1984; Kogan, 1995, 2002), which is a global
kind of identification of the child with his or her damaged parent.
This phenomenon is similar to the identification that takes place
in pathological mourning, which was described by Freud (1917e
[1915]) as a process in which the person in mourning attempts to
possess the object by becoming the object itself rather than bearing
a resemblance to it. This occurs when the person renounces the
object while at the same time preserving it in a cannibalistic manner
(Green, 1986; Grinberg & Grinberg, 1974). Primitive identification
impedes separation–individuation and facilitates the transmission of
aggressive and destructive aspects of the parents' own traumatization, as well as feelings of mourning, pain, and guilt (Kogan, 1995).
The parent's feelings of mourning and guilt become those of the
child, who externalizes them as if they were his or her own feelings.
Survivors' offspring may unconsciously participate in the self-healing

process of the parents and may share their pain and survivor guilt.

There are different types of traumatization that result from "primitive identification" and that are relevant to permeability of boundaries. While the modes of transmission (like projection–introjection) may be universal, in cases of Holocaust survivors' offspring the traumatization bears the unique quality that the Holocaust imparted to it. The patterns of traumatization of the child include:

1. *Traumatization of the child by exploiting him as a vehicle for repeating the parent's trauma.* The damaged parent creates a permeable membrane between herself and the child through which she transmits feelings of mourning and aggression, which because of their devastating nature, she cannot contain in herself or share with other adult partners. This process, which is actually a process of projective identification, serves to decrease the huge amount of self-destructiveness that could have been fatal to the parent (Gampel, 1986, 2005; Kogan, 1989).

2. *Traumatization resulting from the emotional inaccessibility of the parent.* The child who attempts to comfort the parent by catering to her need for total empathy initiates a kind of union with the needy parent in order to nurture her, while actually seeking parenting for himself.

3. *Traumatization through fantasy.* This occurs when the child, in his endless efforts to understand his parent and thus help her, tries to experience what the parent has been through by recreating the traumatic experience and its accompanying affects in fantasy (Auerhahn & Prelinger, 1983). Oliner (1982), who explored hysterical character traits among children of survivors, found the following aspect of hysteria described by Metcalf (1977) applicable to them: "the parental expectation that the child becomes the protagonist in the scenes from the parents' unconscious fantasies—fantasies that are almost always a sadistic distortion of narcissistic struggles for survival with objects from the parents' past" (Metcalf, 1977, p. 259).

4. *Traumatization through the loss of one's self.* The parent seeks the restitution of her lost (often idealized) objects and the reparation of her damaged self by means of a symbiotic attachment to the child. The child, by sharing with his parent the fantasy

of denial of death and the miraculous restitution of the lost objects, sacrifices his own individuality. If we compare this again to the dynamics of hysteria, we find a similarity between the loss of individuality among children of survivors and the "life of substitutions" described by Racamier (1952) or the "absence from oneself" referred to by Khan (1974).

In this book, I use a case illustration of a patient who was the son of Holocaust survivor parents to examine (a) the patient's struggle against mourning, and (b) the impact of transgenerational transmission of trauma on the breaking of boundaries.

a.   The case illustration (Part One) describes both the adaptive and the pathological aspects of the patient's strategies against pain and mourning, as well as the dilemmas of the analyst in this context. The patient was unable to do the work of mourning when confronted with the loss of his son, as he was fixated in a state of pathological mourning throughout his life due to his inability to separate from his maternal object. The journey from manic defences to pain is explored in detail.

b.   The book delves in Part Two into the breaking of internal and external boundaries associated with growing up with parents who were traumatized by the Holocaust. The subject matter is viewed from developmental, cultural, and clinical perspectives.

From the developmental perspective, the book deals with the destruction of outer interpersonal boundaries between generations through an incestuous relationship between mother and son. The impact of this perverse physical and emotional closeness on the son's cognitive and emotional development and on his psychic structure is explored.

The cultural perspective delves into the way the Holocaust affected an entire culture, including the subsequent generations. This is shown by the patient's fantasies and enactments associated with mental representations of the Holocaust. The intrusion of the mother's violent past into the patient's present broke boundaries between past and present, fantasy and reality, self and object. The patient's "flirting" with danger in order to conquer death, his playing the roles of persecutor and victim in his current object-relationships, and his enacting of these fantasies upon his own body are illustrated and discussed.

The book concludes with the exploration of the impact of trauma on the breaking of boundaries from the clinical perspective, and it deals with the patient's breaking of the analytic boundaries of time, place, and abstinence from touch. These boundaries, which represent the reality principle (Freud, 1911b) and are "the guardians of separateness and of the incest barrier at a deeper, unconscious level" (Akhtar, 1999, p. 116), may be regarded by the analyst as an extension of his or her own outer ego boundaries (Epstein, 1994). The book illustrates how the patient used the breaking of analytic boundaries to actualize his craving for oneness with the analyst in his attempt to repeat the incestuous relationship with his mother. Part Two discusses the effect of the patient's breaking of boundaries on the analyst, the intrusion of his son's suicide into the treatment, and how the analyst survived the patient's aggression and dealt with this very complex situation.

PART ONE

CASE ILLUSTRATION

1

The first encounter

David, a 54-year-old engineer, married for the second time and father of three, sought professional help for exhaustion, depression, difficulty functioning at work, and thoughts of suicide.

David was referred to me by his dermatologist, who believed that David's sores "refused" to heal because of underlying emotional problems. David had always suffered from different somatic illnesses. He was told that, as an infant, he had nearly died of diphtheria but survived due to his mother's devoted care. As a young child he was underweight and anaemic and spent several months in a sanatorium undergoing treatment for these conditions. At 18 he developed a severe ulcer, and at age 25 he underwent surgery for a slipped disc, after which he lay in a cast for six months. Later in life he suffered from polyps in his respiratory tract, which developed into a cancerous growth (papilloma) in one of his cheekbones and needed to be surgically removed. At present, he is overweight and suffers from high blood pressure, chronic fatigue, psoriasis, and sexual impotence. He is extremely frustrated with his situation at work and feels that life is not worth living. He occasionally entertains thoughts of jumping off a tall building and ending his suffering.

David looked older than he was. His white hair, mournful expression, and laborious way of moving gave him an elderly appearance.

He spoke Hebrew with a heavy Hungarian accent and, in spite of having lived in Israel for the last twenty-five years, had a poor command of the language. Thus, he still gave the impression of a new immigrant, an outsider.

David was born after World War II to parents who had been physically and emotionally damaged by the Holocaust. David's father left his parents' home in Transylvania and emigrated to Budapest before the war. His father's family—his parents and all of his brothers and sisters, with the exception of one sibling who had escaped to the United States—were killed in the Holocaust. In Budapest, David's father met his mother, the daughter of a prosperous Jewish family. David's father was uneducated and poor, and the mother's family protested against their daughter's choice of husband, considering the match a "misalliance", and disinherited her. When war broke out, the couple, being very poor, sought refuge in "Wallenberg's Houses", an area protected by the Swedish embassy. The mother's family, who lived in the more affluent section of the city, was taken to a concentration camp and never returned. The young couple survived.

David was born under unusual circumstances. He was told that his mother, like so many other women during the Holocaust, had been given injections of hormones to stop her menstrual cycle and prevent conception. When the war ended, David's father took her to Romania, where she received other injections to restore her fertility. In spite of the doctors' pessimistic prognosis, she became pregnant with David. The doctors regarded David's birth as a miracle. After his birth, David's mother became very ill. She later developed cancer, possibly from the initial hormonal treatment, and her health deteriorated greatly. At the age of 54 she committed suicide, following an operation to remove the cancerous growth.

After David's birth, his father learned of the death of his parents and siblings in a concentration camp, and he became depressed and emotionally withdrawn. Thus, David the "miracle child" grew up with a physically ill mother and an emotionally absent father.

The family remained in Romania until after David's birth and then returned to Hungary, where both parents found work. In 1957, with the Russian suppression of the revolution against the Communist regime, the entire area where they lived, including their house, was bombed. As a result of the bombing, David, then 10 years old, suffered a nervous breakdown and had to be hospitalized. He remembered the separation from his mother as the most traumatic element of his hospitalization.

The relationship between David and his mother was a special one. At the end of our initial interview, during which David recounted the story of his life, he said: "There is something I haven't yet told you. It is the biggest secret of my life. I have one last wish—to sleep with my mother!" Seeing the amazed expression on my face, he added: "in her grave". The pleasure David derived from my shock and amazement indicated the perverse nature of the transference relationship from the very start and was predictive of further encounters of this sort.

David saw his mother as the anchor of his life, giving him the strength to overcome its hardships and persevere. She was the dominant figure at home and had a derogatory attitude towards his father, whom David experienced as weak and irrelevant to the family. The father, the weak, castrated figure at home, became a devoted Communist who fought for the welfare of the poor. David knew that his father had been involved in extramarital relationships.

David was a problematic child who developed slowly. For several years, the doctors thought him mentally retarded. He was fat and clumsy and was often rejected by other children. Because he was overweight, he found sports difficult. He suffered from enuresis nocturna until the age of 14. David was very close to his mother, and he slept in bed with her until he was around 17 years old.

David's first sexual encounter was with an older woman, a friend of the family who at the time was his father's lover. He claimed that his mother knew about his relationship with the woman but never interfered. When his father found out about it, he confronted the woman with the truth and attempted to hit her.

A strange misunderstanding occurred in analysis when I listened to David's account of the incident: "When my father heard about it, he wanted to beat her", David said. "She then called me and asked me to help her. She was shouting wildly on the phone—kill your father, kill him!" Not trusting my ears, I asked David, "What did she say? Kill him?" "No," answered David, "she said, 'Calm your father, calm him!'" I felt my misunderstanding of David's words was pregnant with meaning.

Talking about his family life, David described two unsuccessful attempts to escape from Hungary (which we later understood as failed attempts to break away from his mother's grip). The first occurred when he finished high school and became a waiter on a train that criss-crossed the country, placing a geographical distance between his mother and himself. He liked the job, but his mother asked him to give it up and come back home. The second attempt took place after several years of marriage and two children. His wife was a non-Jewish, Hungarian woman from a primitive family. He had married her because she was tall and stout, physically resembling his mother. After several years of marriage, he was no longer in love with her and resolved to leave his family. He went to a football match in the West and decided to remain there. Again, it was his mother who demanded that he return home, and he obediently complied.

At the age of 54, the mother underwent an operation for a cancerous growth in her stomach. The doctors informed the family that the operation had been successful and that she would soon recover, but a few days later she was found dead in her hospital bed. The rumour was that she had committed suicide. David felt that he had missed the opportunity to take leave of his mother. He felt that her death was the loss of his protective shield, leaving him vulnerable and helpless, like a child. Several months after her death, David felt there was no longer anything to keep him in Hungary. He arranged a trip to Germany and, without bidding farewell to his wife and children, went abroad and never returned.

From Germany David emigrated to Israel, where he attempted to embark upon a new life. He soon developed a relationship with a prosperous, well-educated woman. Like the wife he had abandoned, she too bore a physical resemblance to his mother. David divorced his wife and married her. He decided that it would be best for him to make a total break with his former family; by not having any contact with them, he erased them from his life.

David claimed that his new wife abhorred the idea of having children, and as long as they had none they were happy together. But after several years, she changed her mind and even underwent fertility treatment to become pregnant. Finally, she gave birth to a son, Avi. The relationship, which David had described as idyllic, changed completely, their togetherness destroyed by the birth of the child. David described his wife as a demanding, coercive mother who was incapable of giving their son the boundless love he had received from his own mother. Her obsession with order and cleanliness was a constant source of conflict. She had frequent outbursts of anger and would shout furiously at him as well as at the child.

From a very early age, their son had difficulty accepting authority, and David's wife accused David of being incapable of disciplining him. David felt he was playing the maternal role in the relationship with his son, by fulfilling the child's every whim, unable to set any limits. The child was an underachiever in school and a loner. He developed into an angry, schizoid adolescent, who would close himself up in his room for hours and barely speak to his parents. He developed a passion for chess and spent endless hours playing it by himself in his room. David was very worried about him. He claimed that the boy was very much like himself, only more so.

During the Gulf War, while serving in the army reserve, David volunteered for a special unit that would rush to the place where a Scud missile had landed to see whether chemical warfare was involved. David was always among the first to arrive on the scene, omnipotently believing that he would survive even if the bomb had a chemical warhead.

Following in his father's footsteps, his son volunteered for the same army division, which now served in a dangerous area in the Gaza Strip. He was a problematic soldier and had great difficulty accepting authority. He was often in conflict with his officers and had been imprisoned several times for disobeying orders. David was aware that his son was exposed to danger, and he expressed great concern for his life.

2

Phase I:
Breaking analytic boundaries—
the incestuous touch

In the first phase of analysis I became aware of David's concrete way of thinking. David spent much time ruminating over his unhappiness, attributing it mainly to his failure to obtain a managerial position in his company. Elaborating upon the unconscious meaning of his frustrated wishes and expectations over becoming a manager at work, I pointed out to David the great difficulty he had managing (having control over) his own body, as evidenced by the many illnesses from which he had suffered. This interpretation facilitated elaboration of his wish to control that was so important to him. In this regard, David revealed another secret—his enjoyment of sado-masochistic movies and the pleasure he took from watching brutal men tying up, beating, and sexually abusing women. David believed that his current impotence was a result of masturbating while watching these movies. He was addicted, watching the movies at home when alone, or in his office, instead of working. He was turned on mainly by the women who, in spite of being big and strong, were willing to do everything to please their torturers. In the transference, I soon realized that I had become the focus of David's masturbatory fantasies. I was the big, strong woman whom he wanted to torture to achieve sexual gratification. However, I felt that it would be premature at this stage of analysis to give David a transference

interpretation of his sadistic and libidinal wishes in my regard. Instead, I pointed out to him how afraid he was of losing control over
his urges, an interpretation he could readily accept.

As analysis continued, I began to experience David as a torturer.
I shall present some examples of his behaviour that expressed his
unconscious aggression towards me.

> Upon entering my office, David usually paused at the door and,
> unlike my other patients, waited for me to go in first, following
> me from behind. This gave me an uneasy feeling that he might
> attack me unawares. At the end of a session, David would again
> pause at the door of my office, looking me over with apprecia-
> tive glances. David rejected all of my efforts to understand this
> unusual form of behaviour, claiming that he was simply behav-
> ing like a gentleman. In addition, David would hang his coat
> outside my office, on a hanger used by my family, and not on the
> hanger inside my office, as was usually done by my patients. On
> a nonverbal level, I felt invaded by the smell of his very strong
> aftershave, which always made me open the window of my office
> after he left. I felt that David was trying to intrude into my privacy,
> my home, my body. I often tried to make him aware of the ag-
> gression beneath his behaviour, but in vain. "Aggression towards
> you?" he would ask in amazement. "How can you say that—you
> know how I feel about you!" But, in fact, I felt that I knew much
> more about it than he did.

An incident that occurred during this period in analysis greatly
increased my awareness of his unconscious destructive wishes:

> At the end of a session, David got up from the couch and patted
> me lightly on the shoulder. I was dumbfounded, feeling that he
> had intruded upon my "perimeter of safety" (McLaughlin, 1995).
> David left, and I, shocked by his breaking the taboo, tried to sort
> out my feelings. It gradually dawned upon me that David's enact-
> ment was probably a repetition of the forbidden touching that
> took place while in bed with his mother until late adolescence.

David's powerful aggression, which was directed against me, made
me feel helpless and impotent. Could I function as an analyst when
confronted with the destruction of boundaries inherent in his per-

verse behaviour? Was it at all possible for me to work with this patient, and was analysis the treatment of choice for him? I began entertaining great doubts that it was. At this point, Winnicott's (1971) view that the therapist must survive the patient's destruction in order to be used as an object helped me gather the strength to continue treatment.

Gradually, I realized that David regarded me as a figure that embodied both mother/therapist and prostitute. Moreover, I was an incestuous mother, who sexually abused her children. An episode in the transference illustrates this:

> Upon hearing the doorbell ring when the next patient arrived a few minutes early, he said: "This is not an analytic couch, this is a warm bed!" And he immediately added, "I know you have many patients, I am not your one and only." Thus, I was a prostitute who had many clients as well as a mother whose children lay on her couch one after the other.

Only later in analysis could we realize how vital it was for David to be my "one and only". The acting out that followed the above episode revealed more of David's anger and potential destructiveness.

> David was driving back home after the session, when a taxi suddenly obstructed him, forcing him to stop. Despite the heavy traffic behind him, he got out of his car and began shouting at and cursing the stunned taxi driver. David told me that he would have killed the taxi driver that very moment had he had a weapon on him. He was tormented by this incident and felt threatened by his uncontrollable aggression.

In the transference relationship we tried to understand who the man was who had evoked so much anger and aggression in him. Was it possible that I was the taxi driver here in analysis, and he experienced me as obstructing his way? Or perhaps his rage was evoked by the patient who had rung the doorbell at the end of the last session, the person who made him feel that he was not receiving my undivided attention. Did David want to kill all my "sons" so that he could remain my "one and only"?

Little did I know at that time how powerful was David's craving to be my one and only. What I did feel was the mixture of his libidinal and aggressive wishes towards me and fear that he might attack me. At this stage in therapy I asked David whether he owned a gun, which he laughingly denied. I had the feeling that David might have sensed my fear of him and was enjoying it. The series of episodes that followed confirmed my feelings.

> Resuming analysis after the Passover break, David handed me a present wrapped in colourful paper. I opened the package, and inside was a picture of him leaning against a tall column. The picture was in a silver frame with the words "Eiffel Tower" engraved on it. David said, "I thought about you all the time I was in Paris with my family! What a city!" In answer to my question of why he brought me a picture of himself, he replied "This is the only picture in which I appear alone, so I brought it for you!"

David definitely did not want any of his family members interfering in our relationship. I wondered silently to myself whether he brought me the picture because he was uncertain that I would remember him. But what did the column he was leaning against represent to him, I asked David. David was unable to associate anything with it. Could the column represent his masculinity, with which he was trying to impress me? This possibility appeared very remote from his conscious awareness. Was I the column on which he was leaning in analysis? David indicated that this possibility was indeed feasible. If so, I thought, then David was endowing me with the phallic qualities represented both by the column and the Eiffel Tower.

David then proceeded to tell me about an episode of acting out during his vacation which had tormented him greatly.

> He had travelled from Paris to Hungary, his country of origin, to attend a conference. In Budapest he came across a woman who had been a close friend of his parents. The woman shared some personal details of her current life with David, telling him how very concerned she was about her son's life and career and her hurt over his alienated behaviour. David advised her to erase the son from her life, to forget him as he had forgotten his sons from his previous family.
>
> During this encounter, in which David shared some personal details about his own life, he suddenly found himself making love to the woman.

David emphasized that he had never before cheated on his wife and was therefore puzzled by his own behaviour. In the transference I told David that this episode might have been an enactment of his sexual wishes towards me, evoked by the emotional closeness he experienced with me in analysis. This time David had no qualms accepting my interpretation.

David's relationship with his wife was complex and difficult. At the beginning of analysis he claimed that although his wife enjoyed sex, he himself was impotent. However, he now revealed that his wife was quite reluctant to have sex with him. Thus, while in his fantasies he was often a powerful, brutal man, in reality he felt the castrated victim of a dominating, powerful woman whom he idealized. David hid his anger and hatred towards his wife behind this idealization, a mechanism that he also used towards me in analysis.

At this stage of analysis (after a period of one year), David informed me of his desire to stop treatment for financial reasons. My attempt to inquire into the unconscious motives behind this unexpected decision was a total failure. In response to my suggestion that we needed time to understand the reasons for such a drastic act, David said that "he was giving me one month's notice, fair enough for any job". David's aggression and destructiveness were obvious to me, but they were inconceivable to him.

I felt helpless to prevent David from leaving treatment. I understood that he probably wanted to run away from his libidinal and aggressive wishes towards me, an enactment that could be regarded as a repetition of his past attempts to run away from his mother. Unsuccessful in making him aware of his conflicting wishes and fears, I told David that I respected his decision to leave although I did not agree with it, and that I would be here for him should he change his mind. David expressed his gratitude, stressing that he would come back to analysis as soon as he could.

3

Phase II:
Breaking analytic boundaries
of time and place

David never realized his wish to leave analysis. The traumatic event that occurred that same week changed his mind. I shall describe it in detail:

> At nine o'clock in the evening I received a phone call from David saying that he was cancelling his sessions for all of next week. In answer to my enquiry about what happened, he replied in a tone devoid of emotion, "My son committed suicide." "What?" I said, shocked and horrified. "I was afraid this would happen", he answered. "I am not surprised; I will come to my session next week after the *shiva* is over."

("*Shiva*", meaning "seven", is the Jewish mourning period, in which the bereaved remain at home for seven days, usually sitting together in the house of the deceased. During this week, friends and family visit and offer their condolences, share memories, and thus provide emotional support.)

Unfortunately, the following week a tragic event occurred in my own life. My father, aged 96, died after a prolonged illness. I phoned all my patients, telling them that I would be away for the following week for personal reasons. One can imagine my amazement when, during the week of *shiva* in my father's apartment in another city, I opened the door to find David standing there.

> He was wearing a black skullcap on his head, and a beard adorned his face. (It is a Jewish custom that a man does not shave during the first month of mourning. Wearing a *kippa*—skullcap—is a sign of respect to God that is common during mourning, even among non-religious Jews.) He came in and sat down with an ease that was in stark contrast to my discomfort at seeing him. David said: "I saw the announcement in the newspaper and decided to visit you. So you are also in mourning, you are 'sitting *shiva*' like I did last week." (It is customary to put a notice in the newspaper, including the name of the deceased and the name of the family in mourning. Traditionally, the house of the deceased is open to visitors, and paying a visit to the bereaved is considered a "good deed"—*mitzvah.*)

Confronted by David's breaking all boundaries, I felt totally helpless. David's condolence visit to me in my father's home destroyed the psychoanalytic setup, the borders of time and place, as well as the asymmetry existing between us.

> My embarrassment grew even greater when my son, aged 31, came into the room, gave me a kiss on the cheek, and said: "Hi, Mom, how are you?" David looked at him and said, "I am a patient of your mother's", and after several moments added, "My son committed suicide a week ago." I could see the amazement and confusion on my son's face. My son remained for a few minutes, made an excuse, and left. "There was no place for me there," he told me afterwards. David's visit lasted about fifty minutes. At the end of his visit he suddenly exclaimed: "I think that my son did what I wanted to do but didn't dare."

In spite of my confusion and embarrassment, the complete breaking of analytic rules, and the violent intrusion into my life, I was also aware of David's tremendous need to see me after his misfortune and of the fact that I was giving him an analytic session under very strange circumstances.

Working through my own feelings regarding this episode, I had to sort through some difficult questions: Why did David tell my son about the suicide, I wondered. Was he trying to erase my son from my life by implying, "Do the same—vanish from here!" so that David could remain my "one and only"? If he had unconsciously wished to erase his own son from his life, how was he coping now that his wish had been realized by the boy's self-destructive act? The elaboration of David's unconscious wishes and guilt feelings regarding his son's suicide was possible only later in analysis.

4

Phase III:
The manic period—
denial, omnipotence, and sexual promiscuity

The following week David resumed analysis, viewing his decision to stop treatment as no longer relevant. The beginning of this phase was characterized by David's manic defences and euphoric demeanour, which enabled him to avoid pain. Thus, he was preoccupied with the important visitors who came to pay their condolences during the *shiva*, and he also kept himself busy with the special prayers recited three times a day during the period of mourning.

After the first month of mourning was over, David began encountering enormous difficulty in accepting the reality of Avi's death. He felt it unlikely that his son had actually committed suicide, the futility of the act completely unacceptable to him. David raised the possibility that the death had been an accident, since Avi went around with a loaded gun, which was against army regulations. After several months, the army investigation committee completed its inquiry and came up with the bitter truth: Avi was found in the toilet, where he had shot himself in the mouth, and the bullet had pierced his brain. It was clearly a suicidal act that David could not deny. Following these findings, David began presenting all sorts of magical ideas regarding Avi's death. It was impossible for him to accept the finality and irreversibility of his son's death. He was convinced that Avi himself thought he would somehow survive his own deadly shot, in the same way that he himself believed that Avi was not really dead and would one day return.

Unable to deal with his guilt, David offered many hypotheses for Avi's suicide. He projected the guilt upon Avi's officer and accused him of his son's self-destructive act. Apparently, the officer had threatened to put Avi in jail again for disobeying orders. David and his wife had wanted to write "Murdered by his officer" on Avi's tombstone, but the military authorities refused. David also suggested that the suicide might actually have been an altruistic act, to publicly denounce the Israeli army's persecution of its own soldiers. Given this perspective, the self-destruction became an idealized act of strength and martyrdom. At other times David sought an excuse for Avi's act, such as the possibility that Avi had had a high fever or was dehydrated, which could have impaired his judgement and affected his behaviour.

In my countertransference, I felt how hard it was for David to deal with the pain and the narcissistic wound caused by Avi's suicide. At the same time, I found it difficult to witness David's mechanisms of self-deception and his efforts to avoid mourning at all cost. But knowing that these mechanisms were, at this stage, vital for his psychic survival, I was able to respect his defences.

A major obstacle on the road to mourning was the eroticization of the transference and the sadomasochistic game that David began playing. The following example illustrates this:

> David came into my office and, seeing my new lamp, began playing with the dimmer, making the room almost dark. The fear I had felt in the earlier stages of analysis began creeping up on me, as I again experienced David as potentially dangerous. In contrast to the earlier stages of analysis, however, I summoned my strength and spoke to David about his lack of respect for boundaries and his need for controlling the analytic situation. In this regard, I reminded him of his visit to my father's house during the *shiva*. The elaboration of this episode made David aware that he had indeed violated boundaries, but he did not find much wrong with it. He claimed that he, like Avi, had never adhered to rules and that dealing with boundaries was extremely difficult for him. In this context, he recalled the absence of a father who could establish boundaries, and the presence of a mother who set no limits

to the emotional and physical relationship between herself and her son, and who allowed him to sleep in her bed until the age of 17. David stated that he found the boundaries of the thera- peutic relationship difficult. He mentioned that he had tried several times to get closer to me by asking me personal questions about myself, and he felt the wall I had erected between us. He longingly anticipated the analytic sessions, being with me in my office, our discussions. The time boundary—my sending him out into the cold at the end of forty-five minutes—was simply unbear- able. (In this context, Krapf, 1956, p. 300, has observed that the theme of clothing as a "warming" protection comes up frequently in connection with an impending separation from the analyst: "Behind separation there is apparently a fear of 'being left out in the cold'.") "What am I going to do with these feelings?" asked David. "I was like a train travelling towards death, and suddenly a locomotive came and led me in the other direction, towards life." We were quiet for a while and then he said, "You have many patients and I have only you."

In the following sessions David talked about his yearning to be bliss- fully united with the woman he loved, which in the transference was with me. Delving into his fantasies, we discovered that he wished to be with this woman in a kind of bubble, on a deserted island, with no one else around. He could not understand how he had had children from both marriages, as they interfered with the oneness with the woman he loved. In spite of this, his second wife even underwent artificial insemination to become pregnant. David explained that his sperm could not live in the acidic environment of a woman's body, and they therefore died in his wife's womb. If so, I said, perhaps he felt that he had almost died in his mother's womb. "Yes," answered David, "I did almost die there; I have already died many times." In the transference I pointed out to David that he was perhaps experiencing the analysis—my "womb"—as potentially dangerous for him because of my frequent attempts to put him in touch with his overwhelming feelings of pain and his mourning. Is it possible, I asked David, that he was trying to defend himself against what he felt was the "acidic" environment in analysis by infusing it with ideal- ized qualities of warmth and intimacy and was covering his pain and mourning with his erotic wishes? David reacted immediately to my questions: "There is a lot of pain in me and I am in mourning all

the time. My son left a hole. It is impossible to fill it; there is a lot of
death there inside me."

We were quiet for some time, and I felt his heavy burden of pain
and guilt upon my shoulders. Was it desirable to put David in touch
with these unbearable feelings, and, if so, at what cost? And if I were
the locomotive, with the role of changing the train's direction from
its destination to death and leading it towards life, how could I, at the
same time, put David in touch with the death and destruction that
controlled his inner world? Would this awareness not strengthen his
self-destructive tendencies? But, if I let David conceal his pain and
mourning from himself, would they disappear? Perhaps the reason I
was hesitant about helping him get in touch with his pain and guilt
lay with me, I continued to ponder. What was my problem in helping
him acknowledge these difficult feelings?

It gradually dawned upon me that whereas in the earlier stages
of analysis I experienced David as my tormentor and myself as his
victim, by putting David in touch with his feelings of mourning and
guilt, I would become the sadistic, persecutory female (his internal
maternal representation) that he expected me to be, which would
make me a pawn in his sadomasochistic game. This realization was
confirmed in one of our subsequent sessions, which dealt mainly
with David's projection of the persecutory figure of a murderess
mother onto me in the transference:

David arrived at this session looking sad and exhausted, and
complained about his rapidly deteriorating relationship with his
wife. His wife, whom he viewed as very achievement-oriented, was
challenging the army report, which stated that she had placed a
lot of pressure on their son to succeed. He felt that the army was
transferring the guilt and the responsibility for Avi's suicide to
his wife. Was this also a voice inside himself, I asked David. David
answered that his wife was not in any way directly guilty for their
son's suicide; however, indirectly, she might have had a great deal
to do with it. Actually, right now, they were both like trains going
in different directions. He wanted to forget what had happened;
she made him angry by forcing him to constantly deal with his
pain and mourning. I pointed out to David that he might be feeling angry with me for the very same reason. "Angry with you?"
asked David amazed. "You are my mythological mother, you are
a Greek goddess!" "What goddess?" I asked, surprised by his re-

sponse. "Medea," he answered without hesitation. "She killed her children, but what a woman! She slept with all the Gods!"

It was now clear to me that David was projecting his monstrous maternal representation upon me. On the one hand, David identified with the gods who enjoyed the sexual favours of this promiscuous mother; but on the other hand, David was himself the battered child of a murderess mother, a child who was doomed to die at her own hand. Further psychic work was required for David to realize both that he was identifying with this inner representation and that, at the same time that he was experiencing himself as her victim, he also felt he was a murderer. This was apparent from two consecutive dreams that David related during this period.

In the first dream,

David saw Avi alive and coming back home from his army service.

In the second dream,

David and his father were attending a religious ceremony that included people of another religion, possibly Arabs. David's father was dressed as a priest. They brought in the head of a man, in a golden glass bowl. The head was an offering to God. Everyone was praying to this head.

In his associations, David stated that the purpose of this offering was to unite with God. He recalled the biblical story of Abraham's readiness to sacrifice Isaac in order to fulfil God's wish (the "Binding of Isaac", called in Hebrew "*Akeida*"). The story, in his view, showed how far Abraham was ready to go to achieve this union with God. The head in the golden bowl did not remind him of anyone he knew. His father, the priest, was presiding over the ceremony.

Was it possible, I wondered silently, that the head in the glass bowl was David's own head; that perhaps this was a decapitation (or castration), in the presence of a father/priest, which David had inflicted upon himself as punishment for his incestuous cravings for oneness with a mother/goddess? Or, I continued to speculate, had David delegated death by decapitation to his son, Avi, who committed suicide in his stead, David thus committing suicide by proxy?

David raised another possibility in his further associations with regard to the offering to God in his dream. He again referred to the powerful, godlike wife/mother with whom he craved to be united in a blissful union, where he would be her "one and only". He would live with her in a kind of cocoon, without children and without worries. Following these associations, I pointed out to David the unconscious conflicting wishes battling inside him. His first dream expressed his wish to revivify his son and bring him back home. In his second dream, he decapitated his son in order to unite with a godlike figure. In this case, the head in the glass bowl was Avi's, and David perhaps felt that Avi had realized his father's wish to destroy him in order to achieve a blissful union with a godlike wife/mother. If this hypothesis was correct, I thought silently, then reality (Avi's suicide) had given credence to David's murderous fantasies, greatly increasing his feelings of omnipotence and "persecutory guilt" (Grinberg, 1992).

During this period, David began to become obsessed with the possibility that Avi had not really committed suicide, but had actually been killed by others. Shocked by this paranoid idea, I asked David who these "others" who killed Avi might have been, and why they would want to perform such an awful deed. David explained that they were probably Avi's army officers who regarded Avi as a troublemaker and who might have pressured him into committing suicide in order to be rid of him. Apparently, David was trying to ease his feelings of guilt by projecting the blame onto others. It took me a while to understand that what seemed to be an insane, paranoid statement, actually made sense if David was unconsciously including himself in the category of "others". Only later in analysis were we able to delve into David's persecutory guilt over feeling that he was the murderer of his own son.

Attempting to escape his pain and guilt, David's manic behaviour continued. David was offered early retirement at work, which he happily accepted. Having lots of free time and enough money, he registered for an advanced course in his field, joined a fitness club, and worked on plans to establish a chess club in Avi's memory. He became an amusement freak, frequenting the theatre, concerts, restaurants. In the midst of all this, he decided to check out his manhood in a "health club" located on the outskirts of the city; this was actually a brothel, where he received a "full massage" from a young girl. The outcome was a complete failure, but David stressed that "he paid the girl for her time, since she had worked hard on him".

This theme was repeated in another episode:

David participated in an event arranged for bereaved families of soldiers who were killed during their army service. The group was taken by bus to a luxury hotel at the Red Sea, paid for by the Ministry of Defence, to discuss the legal rights of bereaved families. David went alone, as his wife refused to accompany him. He felt like a "bachelor out on the town" and flirted with the women. The food and the wine were wonderful. People sat together in the evening and sang songs. David's description seemed to be more of a party than of families in mourning.

In his luxurious bedroom, David decided to check out the hotel's escort service. Using the internet, he invited a girl to his room and she arrived promptly. He described the girl as being barely 20 years old, too young and too thin for his taste. He was unable to have full intercourse with her, but in spite of that, and maybe even because of it, he was sure that the girl had enjoyed it.

I pointed out to David that he was placing me in the role of the whore with whom he wanted to have an erotic interchange. My transference interpretation had no emotional impact on him. David had no problem acknowledging his desire to have an affair with me; moreover, he talked about his physical relationship with his mother until late puberty as a source of pleasure. "Why shouldn't a son sleep in bed with his mother?" he asked with a smile. "It's forbidden only because of social conventions; otherwise, I don't see anything wrong with it."

An uncanny incident during this period made me feel the power of David's craving for oneness.

As the Passover holiday season was approaching, I informed David that I would be away for the second part of the Passover holiday. (The Jewish Passover lasts for seven days; the first and last days are major holidays; people often go on vacation during this time.) At the next session, David joyfully told me that he and his wife were also going away on vacation a week before us, to a time-sharing hotel in Crete. I was stunned, as my husband and I apparently belonged to the same time-sharing club, and for some time we had planned a vacation in one of their hotels in Crete.

My first reaction was to cancel our vacation, as I was aware of the possibility that I might encounter David abroad. Talking over my dilemma with my husband, I realized that he would be very disappointed to cancel the vacation (it was too late and too costly to make different travel arrangements at this stage). We had both decided some months earlier to vacation in Crete, and he saw no reason to cancel, especially as the time-sharing club had several hotels all over the island and, in addition, my patient planned to fly back to Israel from Crete on the day that we would first be arriving there.

In Crete, I made sure to arrive late at the hotel, to allow for the remote possibility that, should David have been staying at the same hotel, he would already be on his way back to Israel. Fortunately, everything went smoothly. Our arrival was uneventful, although I was aware that I was tense and on guard, lest David somehow spring out of nowhere.

After the Passover vacation, David described to me in detail the beautiful island and its interesting archaeological sites. He also told me the name of the hotel he had stayed in and jokingly added that he now felt one hundred per cent, as he stayed in room number 100.

I was completely astounded and felt the blood draining from my face. This was uncanny! Not only had we spent our vacation at the same hotel, but we were actually given David's room after he and his wife had vacated it. David's incestuous fantasy was realized—mother had indeed slept in his bed.

Following this incident I attempted to elaborate upon my feelings. It was clear to me that David was not to blame, as he could not have been involved in the distribution of rooms to guests in the hotel in Crete. Was I to blame, I asked myself. Should I have cancelled my vacation, as I knew that David was travelling to Crete and that there was a possibility of an encounter? But if I had cancelled my vacation, wouldn't I have felt that my freedom was being curtailed and consequently would resent him?

I realized that by blaming myself I was trying to master the uncanny nature of this event. At the same time, I also became aware of the power of David's craving for oneness, of his ability to know things I had never told him about myself and my personal life. David's powerful fusional needs resonated in me: they reminded me of my own longing for fusion and of my own difficulties with individuation from my parents, who were indirectly affected by the Holocaust.

Another incident, which occurred several months later, made me more aware of this resonance.

> I had returned to work after a summer vacation in Rio where I had attended a psychoanalytic congress in which I received an award for my work on the subject of second-generation survivors of the Holocaust. In the first session after the vacation, David asked me smilingly whether I had received his fax while I was away. "I know that you received an award in Rio", he said. "I searched for you on the internet and found some information about it. I understand that it was connected to your work on the Holocaust. I found the name of the hotel of the congress, but there was no fax number. I had to do a lot of detective work to find it. I sent you a fax congratulating you on your prize." Still amazed by this further breaking of boundaries, I thanked him and added that I did not get his fax, as I had stayed at a different hotel. David mumbled, "Never mind, I was with you anyway at the time."

I was again dumbfounded. It was a fact that in Rio I had chosen to present David's case in its shortened version. I could have presented a theoretical work dealing with my approach to second-generation survivors or a review of my work over the last twenty years. But, as I tend to convey my thinking most effectively by means of case illustrations, I presented the case of David. On a fantasy level, David was with me in Rio.

The painful elaboration of my own symbiotic needs through long years of analysis had made me aware of the negative feelings hiding behind them. Thus, it was clear to me that behind David's wish to unite with me in a blissful union was his hidden wish to destroy my autonomy as a separate person. At the same time I felt that David's craving for oneness had intensified with his son's suicide. Knowing from my acquaintance with him that it would be futile at this point to confront him with his negative feelings towards me, as he would totally reject them, I told David that he was apparently doing everything possible to avoid being in touch with his pain and bereavement. David confirmed this by saying: "Yes, I am just trying to get a good taste of life." Then he continued: "My son was only an episode in my life. I was here in this world before him and I'll be here after him." While this was an accurate statement, its monstrosity made me doubt not only my professional ability to help David work through his mourning, but also my emotional capacity to view him as human. This, combined with the extreme and excessive boundary breaking, made it necessary for me to make a gargantuan effort and summon all my strength in order to remain "alive and whole" (Winnicott, 1971) and resume my therapeutic role.

5

Phase IV:
From manic defence to mourning

The transition from manic defence to mourning began with David's wish to visit the place where Avi had committed suicide. It was extremely important for him to see where his son had spent the last moments of his life. The army acceded to his request and David went to the army base. David raised some difficult questions: Why hadn't anyone noticed what was happening to Avi? Avi's friend, who was serving together with him, claimed that half an hour before the suicide Avi had begged him to shoot him in the head. How could this friend let him walk away with a loaded gun in his hands, and look for him only upon hearing a shot some thirty minutes later? And how did the army know who had pulled the trigger? Was it possible that somebody was indirectly responsible for Avi's self-destructive act, that somebody had convinced him to do it? At the end of the session, wishing to explore my notion that he felt he was a criminal, I said, "It seems to me as if you wanted to visit the scene of the crime." David took a deep breath and said, "Yes, that was the scene of the crime." Then he got up and said: "The question is—how did I contribute to that crime?"

In the period that followed, David's mood changed from mania to deep depression. He lost interest in sports and in his studies and even gave up the plans for the chess club that he had wanted to establish in Avi's memory. He was unable to sleep through the night, and he was extremely irritable and angry. At times he entertained fantasies of leaving his wife and going somewhere in the world where he could begin life anew; other times he expressed the wish to return to Hungary and take his own life and thus, at long last, be blissfully united with his mother. In this regard, David related a story about a colleague from work who was in charge of safety control in a kindergarten.

> This colleague was standing trial because of the death of a child as a result of a fatal mistake made by him. I first asked David if he felt that he had made a fatal mistake in watching out for his son's safety. David's immediate answer was: "Avi committed suicide; my depression certainly had an effect on Avi." David complained that he was obsessed with the thought that a murderer was roaming around freely. It was clear to me that he was unconsciously referring to himself.

> David sounded cross. I then asked him whether he felt that I, the person in charge of his safety, was failing in my role of taking care of him. David's spiteful answer confirmed my hypothesis: this treatment is sheer futility; he feels terribly tired, exhausted; I am not helping him; I never tell him what to do; all this delving into the past is totally useless; he needs some practical guidance. If it weren't for the fact that he wanted to be with me, he would have stopped the treatment ages ago.

This was the first time that David had attacked the treatment verbally. I reacted to David's irritated, bitter tone of voice, saying that I realized how angry he was at me for putting him in touch with his pain, and I stressed that by attacking the treatment he was trying to get rid of me. I added that he was now capable of expressing his anger towards me freely, which was a sign of progress.

Next session David stormed into my office in a terrible mood, relating that he had had an uncontrollable fit of anger the day before.

> He had participated in a ceremony for soldiers who lost their lives during their army service, an event organized by the army. It was a huge gathering—twelve hundred people participated in

it. Everyone had to undergo several security checks, especially as the Chief of Staff was taking part in the ceremony. When the girl at the security gate informed him that he had to remove all metallic objects before they performed a body check, he felt an uncontrollable anger well up inside him, and he began to shriek and sob. He screamed that he was a bereaved father, he had given his son for this country, why did he have to undergo such horrible examinations as if he were a criminal? Several army officials attempted in vain to calm him down. They searched for a doctor to medicate him but couldn't find one. Finally, David went home, wrote an angry letter to the army, and arrived for his session still upset, not understanding what had come over him.

We remained quiet for a while. I then told David that he must have felt humiliated by all the security checks. "Yes," said David, "what do they take me for—a potential murderer?" I was taken aback by David's answer. Who was the girl, I asked myself, who had demanded that David remove his metallic objects (his defences) and undergo a body check? Could it be that the outburst of anger had been directed against me, his analyst, who throughout the treatment had been afraid of his violation of boundaries and his inability to control his violent impulses? Perhaps he experienced my attempts to put him in touch with his unconscious murderous fantasies as an accusation of murder? As if answering my unasked question, David informed me that he wanted to stop treatment. "I want a change, I want to throw away the crutches," he told me with a grin.

In the countertransference, I felt the narcissistic hurt caused by being the "crutches", the inanimate object that David wished to discard. But, attempting to understand him brought several questions to mind. Was his behaviour at this point an attempt to protect me from his own murderous rage and destructiveness? Was it possible that, unconsciously, he felt guilty that his mother had taken her own life? And wasn't Avi's suicide a repetition of the trauma, which strongly reinforced his feelings of guilt, thus convincing him that he truly was a murderer? If so, was it possible that David, afraid that he might destroy me as he had destroyed his mother and his son, felt that he had to leave treatment for his safety and mine?

The answers to these questions were revealed in the next session.

David again began to tackle the issue of his guilt over Avi's suicide. He said, "There is something I've never told you. When Avi deserted his unit the second time, I put pressure on him to go back. I did not want a son who was a deserter. The entire course of events might have been different if I had reacted differently. We will never know."

I asked David whether he felt that my opposition to his desire to desert treatment might endanger his life. This was frighteningly similar to David's insistence that Avi not desert the army, which he felt had ultimately endangered Avi's life. David shocked me by saying: "If there is danger here, then you are in danger. I told you once that if I had a gun, I wouldn't kill myself as Avi did, I would kill someone else. Perhaps that is why you put up all these boundaries between us."

We were quiet for several moments. I felt that David had unleashed his murderous aspect into the room—either he or I could be destroyed. Abandoning treatment was a mild solution compared to a violent acting out that would cause his or my own destruction. However, as a result of the elaboration of my countertransference with regard to David's feelings of guilt caused by the suicides of his son and his mother, I was no longer afraid. I had come to the realization that David's infantile unconscious wishes did not make him an actual murderer. Thus, I was able to summon my strength and say: "I think it is important that you remain in treatment and not leave at this point. Do not be afraid. Neither you nor I will be destroyed. And I hope that when we finish our work, you will be more independent and able to manage on your own."

In contrast to the first time that I had tried to stop David from abandoning treatment, this time I was successful.

David arrived at the next session limping and complaining of back pain. He said, "I came today with all my pain, not in spite of it. I did not want to miss the session. Last session made me understand that you invest a lot of thought in the treatment and that there's a plan for my recovery. This was an important realization for me."

Based on the tremendous amount of work that he and I had done over the years, I succeeded in conveying to David that we could both survive his destructive impulses. My initial fear of David's aggression as well as my belief that he might have induced his son to take his own life had changed, and David was able to perceive this change. Moreover, he could also realize that I had faith in his ability to develop and grow and that I wanted to help him separate from me once he had developed more stable psychic boundaries. The therapeutic relationship was restored, and we both felt that in spite of the problems, our lives as well as the treatment would continue.

David was now ready to delve into his relationship with his complex internal maternal representation. My survival of his aggression in the transference now enabled us to uncover and elaborate upon it. On a conscious level he loved and longed for his mother. Unconsciously, he felt guilty that it was his conception and birth that had caused her illness and her enormous suffering, which was eventually the cause of her suicide. His guilt was reinforced by his unconscious hatred of his mother, who had used him to gratify her needs and then abandoned him through her self-destructive act. Becoming aware that he could also deeply hate his loving, nurturing mother who had fought hard to give him life and to keep him alive when he was an infant was extremely painful to him. For a long time in analysis he tried to cling to his idealized image of her and denied the horror of their perverse closeness. Much psychic work was needed to help David acknowledge the dark aspects of his relationship with his mother. The long, painful work of mourning and the elaboration of his hateful and destructive feelings towards her, as well as towards me in the transference, helped David achieve a greater degree of separation from his mother, thus establishing more stable psychic boundaries.

In contrast to his former wish to go to Hungary to commit suicide and unite with his mother in her grave, David now decided to travel to Budapest to see his sons from his first marriage. He was excited at the prospect and expressed the desire to write a will in which he would leave them his parents' house as an inheritance.

On his return, David reported on the encounter with his sons, which he described as very moving. They were now grown men, appearing almost strangers to him. They had both chosen the Christian faith of their mother, and one of them was studying theology. We connected David's guilt for abandoning his sons with the guilt evoked by Avi's suicide. I reminded David that, in both cases, he had expressed the wish "to erase the children from his life, to live with a

woman in a kind of bubble, without children and without worries."
David replied, "That was only a fantasy. In reality, Avi was very important to me and I worried about him a lot. I loved and admired
Avi very much." I felt that David was now better able to deal with his
destructive wishes because his hatred of his son had been mitigated
by his love for him. David was now able to create a boundary between
fantasy and reality and could better differentiate between them.

At this stage of analysis, David's omnipotent defences were replaced by working through his mourning and guilt over Avi. Now
that he was better able to accept Avi's death, he could cry over his
loss and mourn his son's talent, youth, and beauty. David felt that
in losing Avi he had lost an important part of himself; he was aware
that by renewing contact with his sons abroad, he was attempting to
retrieve other parts of himself that were lost a long time ago.

There was a change in David's relationship with important objects in his life. He spoke about his wife with greater compassion
and empathy. Their relationship improved, although he still had
difficulty functioning sexually. In this regard David mentioned that
he had given up watching sadomasochistic movies, that he no longer
felt the need for them. Although he still felt tired at times, his terrible exhaustion was gone, his blood pressure was stable, and the
psoriasis had healed. With the diminishing of his depression, he
decided to look for work.

In my countertransference, I felt that David was more accepting
of the analytic boundaries. I also felt that his aggression was under
better control, which was an indication that his ego boundaries were
stronger. His craving for oneness with me had diminished, thus establishing a psychic boundary between us, which enabled David to
continue analysis with a more secure sense of self.

PART TWO

THEORETICAL ISSUES
CONNECTED TO THE CASE ILLUSTRATION

6

The struggle against mourning

The two aspects of mourning

In this book, mourning is defined from two perspectives: as a process that occurs in reaction to the loss of an object, and as a process that accompanies growth and change from one stage of life to another.

The work of mourning due to object-loss includes a massive psychic effort to recover a link with reality and to detach oneself from the persecutory aspects of the lost object by assimilating its positive and kindly aspects. Viewing it from this perspective, Burch (1989) regarded it as "a kind of final act of love" (p. 622).

Freud (1912–13) defined the outcome of mourning as follows: "The task of mourning is to detach the survivor's memories and hopes from the dead" (p. 65). Anna Freud (1960) refined this definition by stating that "mourning, taken in the analytic sense, is the individual's effort to accept a fact in the external world (the loss of the cathected object), and to effect corresponding changes in the inner world (withdrawal from the lost object)" (p. 58). Bowlby (1961) saw mourning as the psychological process set in motion by the loss of the loved object and suggested that it usually leads to the relinquishment of the object.

From the other perspective, mourning is a process that accompanies growth and change from one stage of life to another. Pollock (1978) arrived at the conclusion that mourning is not only a process connected to object-loss, but also a process linked to growth and development. Mourning thus is "a universal adaptational series of intrapsychic operations occurring in sequential successive stages involved in the reestablishment of a new level of internal and related external equilibrium" (p. 262). These series of operations are caused by different stages of change that occur throughout a person's development and can be interpreted as threats to one's integrity and self-identity, forcing the individual to suffer deep, painful affects.

Similarly to Pollock, Grinberg (1992) maintained that mourning is not linked exclusively to object-loss; it is also linked to growth and to the passage from one stage of life to another. This process involves the loss of certain attitudes, ways of life, and relationships, which, even though replaced by other, more developed ones, nonetheless evoke pain and mourning. Living therefore necessarily requires that an individual go through a succession of mourning processes that are not always successfully completed.

In this case, mourning due to object-loss included the painful toll on the patient, whether in everyday life or in analysis, as he confronted the loss of his son. Mourning due to growth and change was one of the patient's major problems, as he was unable to go through the normal process of mourning accompanying the dissolution of symbiosis from the maternal object; thus he was trapped in a state of pathological mourning throughout his life.

From both of the perspectives mentioned above—when we are confronted with loss and bereavement, as well as when we pass from one stage of life to another—reality is often distorted or denied. In some cases, neither time nor therapy, perhaps nothing, may completely change this. What was required for recovery in this case was not retribution and triumph, not just the relief of rage, not even simply forgiveness, but an emotional awareness of the loss, genuinely experienced, however painful it was. (Puzzled by the pain of mourning, Freud, 1917e [1915], p. 245, stated: "Why this compromise by which the command of reality is carried out piecemeal, should be so extraordinarily painful is not at all easy to explain in terms of mental economics.") This meant the patient's acceptance both of his vulnerability to loss and betrayal as well as of the vulnerability caused by his own limitations and by the finality of life.

Mourning is necessary because it permits us to relinquish attachments and attitudes that have lost their realistic usefulness, thus facilitating growth and development. By means of the mourning process, the patient strove to accept his losses, overcome manic defences, and readapt his ego to reality. Mourning thus included his shedding of the regressive elements that blocked the way to emotional awareness of psychic pain.

In the next section I examine the concept of psychic pain and then explore denial and manic defences that were employed by the patient to avoid pain and mourning. The journey along the road to mental health included working through these defences.

Psychic pain

The early literature dealing with psychic pain is meagre. Freud (1926d [1925]) introduced the concept into the psychoanalytic literature under the rubric of *Seelenshmerz* [pain of the soul]. His reference was to a child crying for his mother, and he viewed it as analogous to bodily injury and loss of body parts.

Freud regarded psychic pain as a phenomenon parallel to physical pain. In his "Project for a Scientific Psychology", he suggested that this kind of pain resulted from a marked increase in the quantity of stimuli impinging upon the mind, thus causing "a breach in the continuity" (1950 [1895], p. 307) of the protective shield. In "Mourning and Melancholia", Freud related pain to object-loss and compared melancholia to "an open wound" (1917e [1915], p. 253). Later on, in *Inhibitions, Symptoms and Anxiety* (1926d [1925], pp. 169–172), Freud linked his economic explanations to his object-related hypothesis regarding the origins of psychic pain. He suggested that the libidinal energy (cathexis) invested in the longing that is concentrated upon the lost object, and which causes anxiety, is similar to the libidinal energy invested in the injured part of the body, which leads to pain. The prolonged nature of the above psychic process, and the impossibility of halting it, produce a state of mental helplessness that is similar to the helplessness induced by overwhelming pain, hence the painful character of object-loss (Freud, 1926d [1925], Addendum C).

Weiss (1934) continued this line of thinking: "Love objects become, as we know, libidinally bound to the ego, as if they were parts of it. If they are torn away from it, the ego reacts as though it had sustained mutilation" (p. 12).

Grinberg (1964) also referred to the connection between physical and psychic pain, but from the perspective of object-relations theory. He believed that if pain appears in any mourning situation resulting from object-loss, it is because object-loss is experienced by the unconscious fantasy as an attack upon the body-ego; this attack provokes physical pain, which in turn is experienced as psychic pain.

Joffe and Sandler (1965) pointed out a further aspect of psychic pain connected to object-loss. They regarded psychic pain as the discrepancy between the actual state of the self and the ideal state of well-being. When a love object is lost, we not only lose the actual object, but also lose the aspect of our own self that is the complement in us of that object, as well as the well-being that is intimately bound up with it.

Pontalis (1981), too, connected psychic pain with object-loss. Pain stems from the fact that the object is irrevocably lost but eternally retained: "Where there is pain, it is the absent lost object that is present; it is the actual, present object that is absent" (p. 90).

Basing himself on the writings of Khan (1979), Joseph (1982), and Kogan (1990) on this subject, Akhtar (2000) summarized the concept of psychic pain as consisting of "a wordless sense of self-rupture, longing and psychic helplessness that is vague and difficult to convey to others. It usually follows the loss of a significant object or its abrupt refusal to meet one's anaclitic needs" (p. 229).

7

Defences against pain and mourning

Schafer (1968, 1976) claimed that defences have meaningful content, including wishes and fantasies concerning the self and objects. Defences are unconsciously intentional, complex actions with the aim of warding off some unpleasurable affect.

There are many defences aimed at avoiding or controlling pain and mourning. These defences can lead to either healthy or pathological results, especially on a temporary basis and depending upon the individual's overall psychic economy and external environment. Joffe and Sandler (1965) included indignation, de-idealization, and enhanced individuation among the healthy responses to pain, and an attitude of hopelessness and helplessness among the pathological responses to it.

In this book, the patient used denial and manic defences in his struggle against pain and mourning. A brief review of these defences is presented below.

Denial

Denial is one of the main defences employed when an individual is confronted with ageing and death, loss and bereavement, stress and trauma. In its psychoanalytic application, denial is defined as a defence against painful or unpleasurable ideas, affects, and perceptions.

Denial has always been a complex concept, one that has acquired many meanings and connotations depending on the context. In addition to its dictionary definition—"the act of saying no"—the term "denial" and its synonyms "disavowal" and "self-deception" refer to the reality-repudiating aspect of defensive activities and not to a discrete defence mechanism (Dorpat, 1987; Fingarette, 1969; Hilgard, 1949; Weisman, 1972).

Freud (1923e) was the first to describe the denial defence. Using data accrued in psychoanalytic treatment, he hypothesized that some young boys, seeing the absence of a penis in girls, reject the evidence of their senses and imagine that they did see the girl's penis after all. He termed this defensive activity "denial" (or "disavowal").

Early psychoanalytic accounts of denial by Sigmund Freud (1940e [1938]) and Anna Freud (1936) limited the scope of denial to the perception of external reality. Many have disagreed with this restricted view of denial. Klein (1935) viewed denial specifically as one of the important components of manic defence, particularly the denial of the reality of some part of the mind, or of psychic reality. In the same vein, Hartmann (1964), Jacobson (1959), Lewin (1950), and Waelder (1951) discussed the denial of various affects such as anxiety, guilt, and anger, claiming that internal reality may also be denied. From a different viewpoint, Dorpat (1979) argued that denial is the crucial defensive activity involved in the formation of contradictory attitudes.

Denial also has adaptive value (Klein & Kogan, 1986). It was utilized by Holocaust survivors during times of massive trauma, and it may have the function of psychic survival.

Manic defences

Freud (1917e [1915]) described manic defence as a retreat from depression, but it was Klein (1935) who detailed the underpinnings of this defence and Winnicott (1935) who broadened the understanding of it. A large part of the psychiatric and psychoanalytic community evinced little interest in this concept, and although there are many references to it in contemporary literature, only a few authors

(Ogden, 1986; Burch, 1989; Grinberg, 1992; Akhtar, 2001) have explored it comprehensively.

Freud (1917e [1915]) pointed out that the most singular peculiarity of melancholia is its tendency to turn into mania. In such a case the ego apparently supposes that it has dominated the object-loss and is free of the suffering it has had to bear. It then tries to exert omnipotent fantasies in order both to control and dominate objects that have become dangerous and persecutory and also to try to save and repair the objects that it feels it has damaged.

Klein (1935) defined manic defence as a set of mental mechanisms aimed at protecting the ego from depressive as well as paranoid anxieties. She delineated many forms of manic defence and often used the term in the plural. She described manic defence essentially as the individual's attempt to evade the exquisite pain of guilt in the early depressive position. The defence is really a collection of defences involving a denial of psychic reality and therefore of the importance of the objects that are loved and taken in, a denigrating contempt for the objects that are loved so that their loss will not be experienced as important, and a triumphant and omnipotent form of putting everything right. Thus, the ego "endeavors ceaselessly to master and control all its objects", (1935, p. 277) escaping dependency and potential loss.

The constituents of manic defence are, in Klein's view: (1) omnipotence, (2) denial and (3) idealization.

1. *Omnipotence* is the main characteristic of mania. It is utilized to control and master objects, so that a sense of separateness and envy are avoided. Omnipotent defences may create confusion between self and object, and this confusion is expressed through omnipotent narcissistic object-relations (Rosenfeld, 1987) leading to an enduring state of narcissism (Segal, 1983). The illusion of omnipotence, which makes the manic defence effective, derives from omnipotent fantasies that are an essential aspect of the infant's inner world. The destruction of the object in fantasy provides the infant with a mechanism for handling negative experiences and tolerating aggressive impulses. Klein pointed out that by means of the manic defence the subject may destroy his internal objects, but because he is omnipotent, he can immediately resuscitate them (a mechanism called "suspended

animation"). The child's feelings of omnipotence also make mar-
ginal reparation possible in fantasy after aggressiveness has run
its course. Klein regards the disparagement of the objects' importance and the contempt for them as a specific characteristic of
manic defence. As a result, the ego effects a partial detachment
from the objects while at the same time longing for them.

2. *Denial* (reviewed in greater detail above) in this context refers
specifically to the denial of psychic reality. It serves to mitigate
the individual's awareness of his dependence upon others and
also his dread of what may be a persecutory experience as a
consequence of this dependence.

3. *Idealization* is a mechanism that helps to avoid the pain inherent
in ambivalence by a paranoid retreat into separating the good
feelings from the bad. This is achieved by splitting the good from
the bad aspects of the object to create an ideal object and a persecutory one. Idealization tenaciously retains a view of a world
and oneself that is "all good". This, in turn, defends against the
individual's guilty recognition of having injured others, whether
in fact or in fantasy.

The above three mechanisms are interrelated:

> It is typical to find an idealization of the good object so that it
> can be kept as far away as possible from the persecuting bad
> object, and thus avoid confusion with it. This defensive process
> is combined with the mechanism of denial which in its turn is
> backed up by omnipotence: it is omnipotent denial which can
> completely deny the existence of bad objects. In the unconscious
> this process is equivalent to the annihilation of the whole dis-
> turbing object-relationship, so that it is clear that it involves the
> denial not only of the bad object, but of an important part of
> the ego, which is in a relationship with the object. [Rosenfeld,
> 1983, p. 262]

Winnicott (1935) broadened the understanding of manic defence, emphasizing that it is intended to "deny the depressive anxiety
that is inherent in emotional development, anxiety that belongs to
the capacity of the individual to feel guilt, and also to acknowledge
responsibility for instinctual experiences, and for the aggression in
the fantasy that goes with individual experiences" (pp. 143–144).
Winnicott's important contribution was that he ascribed to manic

defence the individual's inability to give full significance to inner reality. It is an attempt to fly away from internal reality, especially if this reality includes depressive anxiety or mourning. In a situation where manic defence is used, mourning cannot be experienced.

Winnicott outlined four components of manic defences: (a) denial of inner reality; (b) flight from inner reality to external reality; (c) suspended animation; and (d) denial of sensations of depression through the reversal of depressive feelings. All of these four components are illustrated in the case illustration described in this book.

1. *Denial of inner reality* involves a repudiation of internalized bad objects, which by becoming generalized, can include the rejection of good inner objects: "Many who live normal and valuable lives do not feel they are responsible for the best that is in them" (1935, p. 133).

2. *Flight from inner reality to external reality* involves omnipotent fantasies that are not so much the result of the inner reality itself as a defence against the acceptance of it. Fantasy thus fulfils an intermediary role between internal and external reality. The flight to external reality in order to avoid a painful internal reality may also take the form of exploitation of sexuality.

3. *Suspended animation*, which refers to omnipotent control of bad internal objects, may also destroy good relationships. As a result, the individual may feel dead inside and the world may appear to be an emotional desert.

4. *The reversal of depressive feelings* and the use of exalted opposites for reassurance are important elements of manic defence.

In his comprehensive exploration of the subject of mourning and guilt, Grinberg (1992) maintained that the manic defence is used especially when depressive anxiety is very intense. Grinberg added splitting to the cluster of mechanisms of manic defence (denial, omnipotence, idealization). In his opinion, manic defence includes all the defences that belong to the paranoid–schizoid position and form a powerful, integrated system directed against psychic reality and depressive experience. Hate, guilt, despair, the need for reparation, ambivalence, and so on, are all denied by means of the manic defence.

A different view of manic defence in contemporary psychoanalysis is that of Ogden (1986). Ogden regarded manic defence as a normal part of development, because the conflict between the pain of dependence and the need for objects is always present in some degree. He described manic defence as an "in-between phenomenon, incorporating elements of the psychic organization of both the paranoid–schizoid and the depressive positions" (1986, p. 84). He contended that everyone relies on this defence to varying degrees in times of difficulty. When dependency needs are an unacceptable part of reality, this defence is mobilized. It returns to the ego the illusion of omnipotence or self-sufficiency. Intensely negative interpersonal experiences that preclude trust render dependency both excruciatingly painful and ultimately unsafe. This impossible situation may be tolerated only through ongoing reliance on the manic defence, in which dependency is abruptly denied.

The journey to pain

In this book I describe a patient who, threatened by fragmentation, mobilized denial and manic defences against pain and mourning as a reaction to object-loss. David's work of mourning was impeded by feelings of depressive anxiety, pain, and "persecutory guilt" (Grinberg, 1992) which flooded his ego, and by the defences he used in his attempt to counteract these feelings. (Persecutory guilt includes anxiety and persecution caused by loss and frustration and it appears in the most regressive states. Grinberg links "persecutory guilt" to the mechanism of the paranoid–schizoid phase, as described by Melanie Klein.) The struggle against mourning resulted in his inability to accept his losses, and in his splitting and denial of reality. David's strategies against mourning had adaptive as well as pathological aspects. They prevented the despair that often accompanies emotional awareness of loss and bereavement, thus helping him survive physically as well as psychically, but also leaving him emotionally depleted. The case illustration highlights David's difficulty in relinquishing his manic defences and my own dilemmas in this context.

From a different perspective, David was stuck in a state of pathological mourning because of his inability to give up his symbiotic needs towards his maternal object. David's emotional experience in analysis enabled him to discover his original attachment and its betrayal and to work them through. Giving up his craving for one-ness with the maternal object, and in the transference with the analyst, was a stage of the mourning process similar to the stages of mourning described by Pollock (1961) and Mahler (1961). The transformation of pathological mourning into normal mourning, which accompanied the dissolution of his symbiotic needs, eventually led to growth and development.

The experience in the transference also enabled David to differentiate between, on the one hand, the Holocaust past of his mother and her suicide and, on the other, his present life and the death of his son. He began to understand that his omnipotent destructive fantasies had no realistic basis. This realization helped him bear the torment of mourning, guilt, and persecution evoked by the loss of his son without fear of being flooded by it. By means of elaborating upon his pain and mourning, he strove to accept his loss and readapt to reality.

David's growing ability to mourn increased his capacity to love and to mitigate hate. The elaboration of mourning eventually led both to a reorganization of the ego and to a smoother interaction between his inner and outer world. Subsequently, his internal world was less denied, and the compulsive need to erase it by manic defences diminished. The mourning process facilitated the integration of the dissociated parts of his self and the consolidation of psychic boundaries, resulting in a better sense of identity (Grinberg, 1992).

8

The impact of trauma on boundaries from the developmental perspective: normal and pathological symbiosis

The healthy aspects of craving for oneness

Longing for oneness is a universal phenomenon that begins at birth and affects cognitive and emotional development. The desire for oneness according to Harrison (1979) has its origins in the infant–mother relationship. Mahler (1972) refers to this phenomenon, as "the mainspring of man's eternal struggle against fusion and isolation" (p. 338). And indeed, symbiosis and individuation are the two poles between which an individual oscillates throughout life (Mahler, Pine, & Bergmann, 1975).

Freud (1930a) called the phenomenon of longing for oneness "oceanic feelings" and considered it to be "the feeling of limitlessness and of a bond with the universe" (p. 68). Milner (1969) called it "a sea of undifferentiated being" (p. 29), and Werman (1986) "a confluence of the inner and outer world" (p. 125). Werman connected this psychic state to an altered state of consciousness. George Klein (1959) noted that such transcendence of consciousness occurs mainly in the emotional state of the artist who departs from mundane awareness and allows for a latent unification with the hidden. Epstein (1990) described "oceanic feelings" as the Buddhist meditation state that recalls "vestiges of primary narcissism" (p. 163). The function of "oceanic feelings" was defined by Meissner (1984) as "a defense against depression and a memory of a buried wound" (p. 48). The concept of "oceanic feelings" has recently been reviewed by Schneider and Berke (in press), who link it to mysticism and Kabbalah.

Expressions of the healthy aspects of the desire for oneness in adult life include love, sexual orgasm, dreamless sleep, rapt absorption in physical exercise, writing and religious meditations, and even longing for oneness with the universe in old age. (In biological symbiosis, two organisms cannot survive without each other. Love can be experienced in a similar way. Symbiotic lovers experience a psychological merger and seem for a time to require no one and nothing else: Person, 1988.) The common tools of analysis—the ability to identify with the patient and be empathic with him—also originate from this wish. The above psychic states involve transient, mind-enhancing, and relationship-strengthening experiences of "oneness" that trace back to early childhood.

I shall briefly refer to the phenomenon of symbiosis from the developmental perspective. (An extensive review of the concept of symbiosis and its connection with object relationships can be found in Pollock, 1964.) Anna Freud and Dorothy Burlingham (1944) reported that the child's feelings of oneness with the mother's body has a parallel in the mother's feeling that the baby's body belongs to her. Benedek (1956) discussed the psychosomatic aspects of motherliness, claiming that the mother had a biological need to continue the symbiosis in the puerperium and during the child's infancy. She felt that the symbiosis that exits throughout pregnancy is interrupted at birth, but that it continues to be a directing and motivating factor in the emotional and somatic interaction between mother and child. Although she focused primarily upon the foetal state and the early period of infancy, she extended the biological concept of symbiosis to the emotional and mental sphere of mother–child interaction after birth. Colby (1949) also suggested that the symbiotic process had its source in biological and psychological needs and that the various couplings, pairings, and fusions of mother and child represent reciprocal interlockings of wishes and defences. Mahler (1952) stated that "the intrauterine, parasite–host relationship within the mother organism must be replaced in the post-natal period by the infant's being enveloped, as it were, in the extrauterine matrix of the mother's nursing care, a kind of social symbiosis" (p. 286). She notes that the bodily contact with the mother, fondling and cuddling, is "an integral prerequisite for the demarcation of the body ego from the nonself within the stage of somatopsychic symbiosis of the mother–infant dual unity" (p. 287). As the child learns about the separateness of its own body contour from that of the mother, he or she achieves a relatively high degree of ego differentiation, an ability to neutralize and direct aggression, and a relatively advanced perceptive awareness of the environment. The child then differentiates between him/herself and the objects in the external world (Hoffer, 1950). Milner (1952), too, wrote about the boundary between inner and outer and its relationship to the feeling of actual body boundary.

If the earlier symbiosis has been adequate, the child is ready to enter the phase of gradual separation and individuation. During the second year of life, it is the maturational growth of locomotion that exposes the infant to the important experience of deliberate and active bodily separation and reunion with the mother. If the mother reacts to the child in a way that does not allow for separation and differentiation, through overstimulation or anxiety, fixation occurs, with subsequent pathology, as I describe further on.

Culture plays an important role in the realm of interpersonal boundaries and craving for oneness. It goes a long way in determining how close or distant well-adjusted individuals may be from each other (Akhtar, 1992). The degree to which a distinct, clearly demarcated, self-observing self—the central subject of psychoanalysis—exists in different cultures varies, to say the least (Akhtar, 1999; Roland, 1988). Consequently, the issue of oneness is to be viewed differently in different cultures.

The pathological aspects of symbiosis

I wish to differentiate between the desire for oneness that belongs to the human experience (described above), and the pathological aspects of symbiosis. The emphasis upon *oneness with the other* overlooks another type of oneness—that is, *oneness within oneself* (Cohen, 2006).

In the case illustration, we encountered a pathological desire for symbiosis of a fragmented self and a constant attempt to escape from selfhood. The patient's pathological desire for symbiosis was caused by growing up with traumatized, damaged parents. The contribution of a mother's pathogenic role in the child–mother relationship to the later difficulty in the adult was described by Khan (1962). It is true that not all children show direct reactions to their mothers' symptoms, but some are affected indirectly only insofar as the mother's illness interferes, or has interfered, with her capacity for effective mothering (A. Freud, 1960).

The effect that trauma can have on mothers and on their relationship with their children was described by Welldon (1993). She suggests that the opportunity that maternity offers to have complete control of a situation creates the right preconditions for certain women, who have suffered harmful traumatic experiences, to exploit and abuse their children. In the above case, the mother appears to have related to her son as a part or prolongation of her own body, which would have served to counter her fear of loss and destruction by creating the illusion that she and her child would remain bound together forever. In this connection, Modell (1961) noted that if the object is not separate, it cannot be lost or destroyed, as it is a part of the self.

Mahler (1952) described this pathological lack of separation in the following way: "The adult partner very often seems to accept the child only as long as it belongs as a quasi-vegetative being, an appendage, to her or his body" (p. 293). Examining the impact of this kind of symbiosis on the child, she claimed that in such cases, the child cannot distinguish between the self and the mother because of a particular overstimulation, resulting in a lack of direction of the libidinal and aggressive impulses. "Both the mother and the self are confused and fused as the goal of unneutralized instinctual forces" (p 300).

Halberstadt-Freud (1989, 1991) also explored the impact of pathological symbiosis on the child. In her view, a symmetrical symbiosis between mother and child is a parasitic relationship built on mutual illusion, as symbiosis must of necessity always remain an illusion in humans. Using the concept of "symbiotic illusion", she claims that a two-sided dependence in the mother–child dyad can lead to perversion.

Burlingham, Goldberger, and Lussier (1955) maintain that the mother's grip on the child who was seduced by the mother's manifest actions, and who therefore had to contend with the actual bodily stimulation and excitement that are aroused by them, is stronger than that on the child who was seduced only by mother's fantasies. The pathology in this case resulted from the conflicts induced by the mother's exploitation of the normal symbiotic ties for her own needs, in reality as well as in fantasy. In reality, the child was excessively stimulated, unable to discharge this kind of stimulation, and unshielded from this hyper-excitation. On a fantasy level, the incestuous relationship between mother and son included the mother's fostering of the child's false belief that he is able to satisfy all her needs, is more important than her husband, and is totally indispensable for her emotional well-being. The child thus believed in an imaginary world where he, instead of being too small and impotent to satisfy her sexual and emotional needs, could do both. Thus, feelings of impotence in the child were warded off by his fantasy of being at one with his mother.

As a result, the child experienced separation from his mother as traumatic. When the child was first confronted with separation (at the age of 10 years), the illusion of symbiotic omnipotence was threatened and severe panic reactions occurred. Additional failures of the attempt to separate continued on into adolescence and adulthood, greatly impairing individuation.

Moreover, the patient's inability to individuate and achieve a separate existence throughout his life hindered his normal development and made him the "secret bearer" (Micheels, 1985) of the mourning and guilt of his mother, thus increasing his self-destructive forces.

In the present case illustration, the breaking of the outer interpersonal boundaries resulting from symbiosis affected the cognitive and emotional development of the patient as well as his psychic make-up. The patient's difficulty in extricating himself from the symbiotic relationship with the mother and creating boundaries around his self threatened the integration of the self (Mahler, Pine, & Bergmann, 1975) and created problems with his body image (Apprey, 1991; Blum, 1996; Brenner, 2004; Fischer, 1991, Kramer, 1983, 1991, 1994; Steele, 1991). The incestuous relationship—which often leads to disturbances in attachment (Bowlby, 1973)—and the parent's failure to mirror (Winnicott, 1967) and reflect the child's experience (Denett, 1987; Fonagy, Steele, Steele, Moran, & Higgitt, 1991) led to several developmental failures in the patient, which I now describe in brief:

1. *Impaired ego-structure.* The disturbed mother–child relationship led to an interpermeability of the ego with the id, a lack of distinction between primary and secondary processes, the persistent dominance of the pleasure principle, and the fusion of inner and outer reality. It also led to a disturbed reality-testing. David regarded his molestation by his mother as an act of love rather than a narcissistic exploitation of him for her own physical and emotional needs. He viewed their relationship as mutually beneficial (Brenner, 2004; Rachman, 1989, 1997). Another result of the regressive fusion between child and mother was that the child's/patient's mental representation of the mother was not sufficiently separated and differentiated from his self, the ego maturation did not advance, and the early symbiotic organization was repetitively sought with objects similar to the original one.

2. *Identification with the victim/aggressor aspects of his mother.* In his family life, David enacted the victim aspect of his mother by playing the role of the battered child of his dominant controlling wife, thus placing her in the role of Nazi persecutor. In his masturbatory fantasies, he was the aggressive adult (the Nazi torturer) who abused the child.

3. *Adolescent suicidal strivings.* The longing to achieve a blissful union with his mother by committing suicide—a longing that is typical of adolescence—was a pivotal component of the patient's psychic life. The association between this longing and thoughts of suicide, or the actual suicide itself, is usually mediated by changes in ego functions, the quality of which depend greatly on the structural–cognitive development that takes place in adolescence (Erlich, 1978). In this case, adult thoughts of achieving a blissful union with the mother by means of suicide had not undergone successful transformation because little had changed in the patient's concrete style of thinking since adolescence.

4. *Defective superego.* In a letter discussing the work of Ferenczi and Rank, Freud (Open letter, 15 February 1924, in Jones, 1957)

associates the wish to return to the mother's womb with the incestuous wish. In his view, the punishment for incest—castration anxiety—is connected to the anxiety of "never being able to return to the mother's body". At the same time, the father, an obstacle to this twofold desire, becomes identified with reality. Freud writes: "Obstacles which evoke anxiety, the barriers against incest, are opposed to the fantastic return to the womb: now where do these come from? Their representative is evidently the father, reality, the authority which does not permit incest" (p. 8). In the case of David, his defective superego stemmed from (a) a weak paternal introject, who was unable to erect any barriers against incest; and (b) the denial by all of the complicity fostered between mother and son in their seductive and sexual transgression, which contributed to the corruption of the son's superego (Blum, 1973).

5. *Perverse psychic structure.* The erasing of the differences between the generations described in this case illustration, which is typical of perversion, has been amply explored by Chasseguet-Smirgel (1978, 1984). She refers to a craving for oneness with the mother as a longing for "union with a universe without obstacles, without roughness or differences, entirely smooth, identified with a mother's belly stripped of content, an interior to which one has free access" (Chasseguet-Smirgel, 1996, p. 77). This phenomenon includes a return to an undifferentiated state that precedes the introduction of separation, distinction, and paternal law and that is specific to the anal–sadistic stage to which the pervert regresses. In this case illustration, we observe this phenomenon in the patient's fantasies of erasing all obstacles (his father, his children, my other patients) that hindered his symbiosis with his mother/wife/therapist. In contrast to the neurotic, for whom the oedipal prohibition is accompanied by a sense of horror—a sacred prohibition, as Freud (1939a [1937–39]) calls it—of returning to the place he came from (the mother's womb) for fear of losing his hard-won identity, in the above case this fear was absent.

The patient did not experience incest as a horror but, instead, idealized the object of his craving. He even consciously identified with his idealized mother through the unlimited love he gave his son.

This idealization led to the blurring of internal boundaries between two intrapsychic structures (the ego and the ego-ideal), which often occurs in children of traumatized individuals and which is characteristic of a "perverse character" (Chasseguet-Smirgel, 1984).

In both erotic episodes with whores described above (see chapter 4), David mentioned that the whore was a young girl. Through the perverted scenarios he created in his mind in these encounters, David may have been enacting the trauma of his childhood. He, the older man, was playing the role of the mature parent who was sexually abusing the child, thus identifying with his mother. At the same time, he converted his infantile trauma into an adult triumph (Stoller, 1975). By reversing these roles in analysis, David was trying to turn me into the idealized mother who would sexually abuse him, thus repeating his childhood trauma.

David used sexuality as a manic defence against mourning. In addition, his masturbatory fantasies provided the illusion of being big, potent, and powerful. They were designed to protect him from massive anxiety and fear of engulfment, as well as to deny his fears of annihilation, disintegration, and loss of identity.

6. *Impaired gender identity.* David's sexual identity was fluid; he identified both with the brutal man as well as with the submissive woman, as a result of growing up with two damaged parents. To imagine a blissful symbiosis, in which being together with the mother is what was needed in order for him to be happy, he had to transform his hate into love. This created a false idyll, which even the death of the mother did not change, because it was not the real but the internal imaginary mother in the mind of the child/patient, who intruded upon and engulfed the self. There were no limitations imposed by the paternal figure. The child thus created his own laws, as his conscience did not forbid him to be the object of his mother's desire and to exclude the father. Deprived of the necessary identification with the father, the child failed to go through normal oedipal development and develop the appropriate symbolization. Castration thus remained a real threat instead of a mere fantasy, because he had failed to comply with the taboo of incest. As the symbolic oedipal father was absent, the difference between the generations remained unclear, and gender identity was not well established. The patient's

individuation and the formation of gender identity were both hampered, with a consequent lack of self-esteem in the child. This situation created a severe underlying depression, a feeling of helplessness, hopelessness, and loneliness. (Impaired gender identity as result of pathological symbiosis was examined in depth by Halberstadt-Freud, 1989.)

9

The impact of trauma on boundaries from the cultural perspective

Reliving the past in the present

A culture may be defined as a particular society or civilization, especially one considered in relation to its ideas, its art, or its way of life (*Collins Cobuild English Language Dictionary*). The Holocaust affected an entire culture, including the following generations. For children of survivors, no matter where they live, there is no escape. There is no memory of a time when the Holocaust did not exist in their awareness. Their "remembrance" of the Holocaust is constructed out of stories—those that were spoken aloud, told and retold, as well as those that were silently borne across a bridge of generations (Auerhahn & Laub, 1998; Axelrod, Schnipper, & Rau, 1978; Barocas & Barocas, 1973; Kestenberg, 1972; Klein, 1971; Laub & Auerhahn, 1993; Laufer, 1973; Lipkowitz, 1973; Rakoff, 1966; Sonnenberg, 1974). Brenner (2002) reports how certain children "enter a psychological time tunnel" and weave their parents' past into their own developmental experience (p. xiii). The children who become burdened by memories that are not their own (Auerhahn & Prelinger, 1983; Fresco, 1984) often echo the drama existing in their parents' inner world by enacting it in their current life (Kogan, 1995, 1998,

2002; Krell, 1979; Laub & Auerhahn, 1984; Phillips, 1978; Volkan, Ast, & Greer, 2002). These violent enactments may be the result of death wishes, which lead them to expose themselves to situations of external danger.

The role that historical processes play in the lives of the ancestors in shaping the offspring's symptoms and character formation has been examined in depth in the psychoanalytic literature. This examination led to the generalization that after shared massive trauma, some transgenerational transmission of its images does occur. These images become intertwined with the core identity (an individual's subjective experiences of his or her inner sameness while sharing certain characteristics with others: Erikson, 1956), and self-representation (the metapsychological reconstruction of an individual's self-concept) of members of subsequent generations in the groups for which the trauma is a historical legacy (Kestenberg & Brenner, 1996; Volkan, Ast, & Greer, 2002). My own exploration of the role of historical processes focuses on the examination of the impact of the traumatic Holocaust past of parents on the lives of their children (Kogan, 1995, 2002, 2003, 2004).

As I have shown in various case illustrations, history is never properly over. That is, the past is never dead; it lives in the mind, never to perish. Turner (1938) eloquently described the intermeshed nature of past and present by considering the present to be the undeveloped past and regarding the past as the undeveloped present.

This connection between past and present derives from the difference between the "facts" of history and the meaning and significance that we attribute to these facts. The initial fact has many ramifications and is not a thing unto itself with sharp and clear outlines. Becker (1955) posed three questions about historical fact: the what, the where, and the when of it. Regarding the *what*, Becker states that historical fact is not the past event, but a symbol that enables us to recreate it imaginatively. As to the *where*, Becker places it in the mind and insists that a historical fact is—not was. While the actual past event is gone forever, it is remembered; it is the persistence of records and memories, rather than the ephemeral event, that makes a difference to us now. He then addresses himself to the *when* of historical fact by claiming that if the historical fact is present, imaginatively, in someone's mind, then it is now a part of the present.

In the case of Holocaust survivors, the historical past is always present. As a result of their traumatization, they often create personal myths and fantasies—a "mythos of survival" (Klein, 1981; Kogan, 1995)—which differ from other types of neuroses. This mythos contains memories from the past, and its function is to maintain a traumatic screen (Kris, 1956)—that is, hiding massive amounts of ambivalence and hostility that can be unleashed by brutality, anxiety, or emotional pathology. This longitudinal process that began during the Holocaust continues to influence the survivor at different stages in his life cycle. It affects his perception of his body image, his object relations, his political views, and the way he relates to issues of life and death. The "mythos of survival" is the realization of conflicting emotions and unconscious wishes regarding living or dying; it often permeates boundaries between generations and is unconsciously transmitted to the next generation by processes of projection–introjection. As a result, the death wish, as well as the struggle against it that existed in the lives of the parents, may become a compelling need in the lives of the offspring.

The case illustration reveals the secret perverse world of the patient, in which the violent Holocaust past of the mother intruded into his present life and broke boundaries between past and present, fantasy and reality, self and object. The conflict between his life and death wishes can be demonstrated by the analysis of the following episodes:

- It is possible that the patient's depression and his own suicidal wish may be due to the fact that he introjected these feelings from his mother and carried them for her during his life. This took on various expressions, such as the patient's suicidal wish to jump off a tall building. To counter this wish, he attempted to infuse his inner life with the perverse fantasy of brutally torturing big, strong women. This fantasy was actually a "manic defence" (Klein, 1935; Winnicott, 1935), which served to overcome his death wishes.

- A further expression of the conflict between life and death forces was the patient's flirtation with danger, which was facilitated by the life-threatening external reality in Israel. In the case of Holocaust survivor's offspring, life-threatening reality does not only reactivate a simple recollection of traumatic events; it also reactivates in the offspring the mental representations of the Holocaust that they share with their parents. These may include real events of a traumatic nature, conscious and unconscious fantasies regarding these events, intense feelings of mourning and guilt, and defences against unacceptable feelings such as shame, guilt, or aggression (Kogan, 2004; Moses, 1993; Roth, 1993).

• By volunteering to serve in a special army reserve unit during the Gulf War, and being among the first to arrive at the site where a Scud missile had landed to determine whether it had a chemical or biological warhead, David was attempting to come close to death in order to overcome it. In addition, he was trying to repair the narcissistic hurt caused by the humiliation and destruction that was inflicted upon his mother's family, who, during the Holocaust, went like "sheep to the slaughter".

• The pull between the forces of life and death was also conveyed in the patient's unconscious perception of the life-giving sexual relationship between his damaged ("dead") parents. Seeing it as "empty" (Ogden, 1966) and murderous (David's description of "the acidic environment of a woman's body"), David fantasized that he had already died in his mother's belly. In order to feel alive and to infuse life into an empty primal scene as well as into himself, he flirted with danger by entering the site where Scud missiles had landed.

• The conflict between life and death forces was possibly further demonstrated by the patient's psychosomatic diseases, with David turning his aggression against himself and expressing his pain through his body.

It should be noted that there is a controversy in the contemporary psychoanalytic literature over psychosomatic symptoms and whether they are the result of an autoimmune response or the implantation of the death drive. Gaddini (1972) claims that psychosomatic outbreaks are non-specific manifestations of chronically unmentalized inward aggression and might be experienced as overwhelming, and Akhtar (2001) stresses the importance of the autoimmune system as the key to the puzzle of psychosomatic symptoms. McDougall (1989), on the other hand, believes that psychosomatic illnesses are related to the death drive and are a means of dispersing an excess of painful emotional experience in the absence of a soothing maternal introject. Emotional experience is ejected rather than repressed, in order to survive psychically. She argues that there exist "unsuspected death-like forces that are apt to pass from one generation to another and may communicate, even to young infants, the conviction that their destiny is to accept non-existence as separate beings in their parents' eyes" (p. 89). These death-like forces may be expressed in psychosomatic illnesses.

While I believe that a suffering organ is undoubtedly due to hereditary, constitutional, and coincidental factors, and it is plausible that they may be connected to a pathological separation from an intrusive object (Kuchenhoff, 1998), in my view, psychosomatic symptoms may also be the result of unconscious fantasies connected to conflicting emotional wishes about living or dying. This is especially true in cases in which the child is denied autonomy by a mother who opposes his psychic separation by using him as a transitional or counter-phobic object for herself, as is often the case with Holocaust survivor mothers. This seems to be amply expressed in the case illustration. From this angle, David's various psychosomatic conditions (psoriasis, high blood pressure, impotence, an ulcer), which represented his self-destructiveness, may be viewed as an enactment upon his own body of his unconscious fantasies regarding his mother's traumatic past. These fantasies may have been acted out by his associating parts of his body with the offending object (the Nazi aggressor) and then attacking them brutally.

• Yet another expression of the conflict between Eros and Thanatos may be seen in the way David related to his mother's anti-fertility treatments. The hormonal injections against conception that the patient's mother received during the Holocaust may have been eroticized by him, and they could have served as a source for his masturbatory fantasies. In these fantasies, he played the role of the brutal male (the Nazi torturer) who performs the anti-fertility treatment, as well as the female victim who underwent it. The fact that he became impotent may be regarded as a form of symbolic self-castration, a punishment for the sadistic sexual wishes towards the mother embodied in these fantasies.

The interplay between present trauma and past trauma

The reaction of Holocaust survivors' offspring to current traumatic events may be severely affected by their conscious and unconscious fantasies connected to traumatic events in their own past as well as to their parents' traumatic past.

To assess how the trauma of the son's suicide affected the patient, we have to understand first how the patient associated this present trauma with his underlying destructive fantasies (of erasing all obstructions to his merging with his wife/mother) and then how this present trauma affected the memory of the past (in this case, how the son's suicide superimposed itself on the mother's suicide).

Greenacre (1967) maintains that in situations in which actual traumatic experiences are associated with an underlying fantasy stemming from difficult experiences, the impact of the actual trauma is more intense, and the tendency to fixation is greater than in instances where life experiences are bland and incidental. In the same vein, Anna Freud (1967) writes: "External traumas are turned into internal ones if they touch on, coincide with, or symbolize the fulfilment of either deep-seated anxieties or wish fantasies" (p. 24). David associated the loss of his son with his aggressive wish of ridding himself of any obstacles to his fusion with his wife/mother. As he had regarded his son as one of these obstacles, he was convinced that he was his son's murderer, the son's suicide perceived by him as the actualization of his omnipotent destructive fantasies. This led to unbearable feelings of pain and guilt that impaired his work of mourning and caused him to turn his aggression against his own self, making him depressed and suicidal.

In the case illustration, the son's suicide also reinforced the patient's prolonged feelings of guilt towards his mother. There is no time in the unconscious (Freud, 1915e), only the articulation of meanings (Schaeffer, 1980). Past and present merge in the unconscious, so that meanings that were still are, and the meanings that are affect and change those that were (Loftus & Loftus, 1980). The psychoanalytic model of trauma is thus composed of two events: a later event that causes the revivification of an original event, which only then becomes traumatic (Laplanche & Pontalis, 1967).

In describing this process, Garland (2002) states that the central difficulty with a disaster lies in the intense struggle to deal with the flood of unmanageable material "in the absence of the apparatus of thinking" (p. 18). Garland states that this is what locks the unmanageable material powerfully and precisely to whatever has been released by the breaking down of internal barriers and structures. She claims that the traumatic influx of stimulation from the present stirs up the early fantasies of devastation and cruelty and paranoid views of relations between objects, which then get bound with present events in a way that is hard to undo. It seems that the more intense and long-lasting the traumatic event, the greater and more lasting the emotional loading that it carries, which makes it still harder to disengage from the newly released and highly charged material to which it gets attached (Garland, 1991). In such instances, what Freud (1920g) might have called "binding" seems to intensify and become a kind of fusion. The past and the present become indistinguishable: each not only makes sense of the other, but each seems to confirm the most pathological features of the other.

David felt in his unconscious fantasy that his conception and birth had led to his mother's illness, suffering, and eventual suicide. This fantasy took on traumatic proportions when reality gave it credence through his son's self-destructive act. David associated his fantasy of being responsible for the trauma of his son's suicide with his underlying fantasy of responsibility for his mother's suicide. The interplay between the past trauma and the present trauma reinforced each of the traumas, convincing the patient that he was the murderer in both.

David may have felt responsible for offering his son to God (see his dream), as in the "*Akeida*" (literally, "binding", the binding of Isaac, the son of Abraham, for a sacrifice), where Abraham almost kills Isaac to satisfy God's wish. This brings to mind the origin of the word "Holocaust". It derives from the Greek word *holokauston*, a translation in the Septuagint for the Hebrew word "olah", which means "what is brought up", "an offering made by fire unto the Lord", or a burnt offering (Bergmann & Jucovy, 1982). This definition interestingly connects the Holocaust past of David's mother with his "*Akeida*"-like dream, possibly indicating that David was superimposing the guilt he felt regarding his son's suicide on the guilt he felt regarding his mother's suicide, thus overlaying one trauma upon another and enhancing each. It was only through the elaboration, much later on in the transference, of his emotional experience that the patient could work through his guilt feelings and realize that he was not a murderer.

10

The impact of trauma on boundaries from the clinical perspective

In their book *Boundaries and Boundary Violations in Psychoanalysis*, Gabbard and Lester (1995) state that "a central paradox of the analytic situation is that professional boundaries must be maintained so that both participants have the freedom to cross them psychologically" (p. 42). In our case illustration, it became repeatedly difficult to maintain the professional (external) boundaries that constitute the analytic frame, within which "the patient's needs, wishes and demands for transcendence and transgression unfold and are understood, renounced, modified and rechanneled" (Akhtar, 1999, p. 116).

In this chapter I discuss the patient's breaking of clinical boundaries with regard to its impact on the analyst and on the treatment when traumatic reality intruded into analysis and broke the boundaries between the internal and external world. In both instances, I discuss how I coped with these problems.

Analysts are continuously attending to the difference between what transpires within the patient and what transpires within themselves. The analytic boundaries facilitate this process by functioning as interpersonal boundaries. The analyst may thus regard them as an extension of his or her own outer ego boundaries (Epstein, 1994), and if the analytic frame is attacked, the analyst might experience it as an attack upon him/herself.

The patient at times appeared submissive and helpless, yet his frequent breaking of the analytic boundaries caused me to experience him as a powerful, menacing figure who could destroy me as well as the treatment. My fear of him made me realize that beneath his game-playing in his relationship with me lay a terrible destructiveness, which included his wish to destroy my separateness and autonomy. I experienced his breaking of interpersonal boundaries as a threat to my safety. There were points in analysis when I asked myself whether I could continue analytic work with this violent, frightening patient. I had to overcome this fear in order to understand my patient. My internal boundaries had to become permeable enough so that my countertransference feelings could cross them, enabling me to be in touch with these feelings and work them through. I could thus retain my analytic function and continue analysis. For example, as I worked through my shock and amazement at the patient's breaking of the analytic boundaries, I became aware of the patient's own fear of his uncontrollable aggression and possible fragmentation. Elaborating upon my anger at his attempt to have sadistic omnipotent control over me by breaking the boundaries of the analytic setup, I understood that this was his way of defending himself against the danger of fusing with me and losing his own self in the process. Analysing my feelings of being under constant stress in this treatment helped me realize that the patient, as the child of two damaged parents, had lived from an early age in a state of chronic "strain trauma" (Kris, 1956). Thus, perhaps he was letting me feel the strain he had experienced in his childhood from being frequently and chronically flooded with anger and sexual arousal without adequate parental protection for modulating these affects. (Pollock, 1964, has described various pathological relationships that reappear in the analytic situation. These are regressive repetitions of the past as they existed in the context of object relationships.)

The craving to merge with his mother, which persisted throughout the patient's life, was expressed in analysis through "transference perversion" (Etchegoyen, 1977). This type of transference includes a narcissistic object-relation, by means of which the patient attempts to construct a delusional subject–object unity as well as to break analytic boundaries. Its aim is to provoke fear and arousal in the analyst. To deal with this "transference perversion", I had to develop a unique form of psychoanalytic empathy towards my patient. This included, in Kernberg's (1995) terms, creating a "thickness" in the treatment's external boundaries by firmly maintaining the therapeutic role, and creating an optimal "thinness" in my internal boundary—that is, an openness to explore unconscious processes and countertransference feelings.

Analysing my countertransference feelings, I realized that in addition to the patient's breaking of analytic boundaries, the overwhelming reality of his son's suicide intruded so violently into the treatment that it erased the boundaries between fantasy and reality for both members of the analytic dyad. I felt threatened because I myself perceived the patient as a monstrous father who might have induced his son to commit suicide, thus fulfilling his unconscious aggressive wishes of erasing his son from his life. My associations with regard to the patient revolved around the legend of Chronos (Hesiod, *Theogonia*: Evelyn-White, 1914, pp. 137–182, 453–506), the Greek god who swallowed his children, and Saturn, another Greek god identified with Chronos, whom Goya in 1820 painted swallowing one of his children. These associations made me aware of how appalled I was by the patient and afraid of his murderous impulses, which I felt had been realized by his son's suicide. Only by working through my feelings did I understand that my own ability to symbolize, as well as the patient's, had been greatly impaired by the traumatic reality of his son's suicide. It was essential that both the patient and myself understood that his unconscious aggressive wishes towards his son (or towards me in the transference) did not necessarily turn him into a murderer. Recovering my ability to symbolize, and to relate to his murderous wishes as an infantile fantasy and not as reality, created a new analytic space in which the patient was no longer a threat to me, and in which we could work through the mourning for his son as well as for his mother.

In this newly created analytic space I was able to show the patient that his breaking of the analytic boundaries, his need to control the situation and destroy the asymmetry between us, and his eroticization of the relationship not only served to rid himself of his painful feelings regarding his son, but also to rid himself of me in my role as therapist. David attacked the treatment because therapy itself was experienced by him as a boundary, a "third", that interfered with the dyadic incestuous relationship he wished to create. My surviving his attacks helped David to better differentiate between fantasy and reality and feel less threatened by his infantile aggressive and libidinal strivings (Kogan, 1990, 2003).

From an entirely different perspective, I would like to mention another aspect of my own countertransference to this patient. The patient's symbiotic tie to his mother and his difficulty to individuate, which is typical of Holocaust survivors' offspring (Freyberg, 1980; Kogan, 1995), resonated in me: it reminded me of my own longing for fusion, and of my experiencing individuation as destructive towards my parents, who, after the traumatic separation from their original families during the Holocaust, could not sustain any more "losses" in their lives. Thus I realized that we shared a common traumatic historical experience on a personal level, as we both belonged to the same large group whose parents were affected, either directly or indirectly, by the Holocaust (Blum, 1985; Kogan, 2003; Volkan, Ast, & Greer, 2002). The trauma of the Holocaust, the havoc and destruction it wreaked upon the lives of our parents, affected both of us, patient and therapist alike. The elaboration of my feelings in relation to this issue enabled me to free myself from identification with the patient in this realm and to perform my analytic role.

Working through the feelings of pain and guilt for his lost son helped David dissociate these feelings from the guilt and unresolved mourning for his dead mother, and it facilitated the restoration of boundaries between fantasy and reality, past and present, self and object. After years of hard work, the patient emerged from the treatment with a better differentiated self and renewed life forces.

11

Special clinical dimensions of the treatment

I would like to refer to several additional aspects of the treatment described in this book:

1. *The analyst's "survival"*. Salvaging my analytic ego and continuing to function as an analyst—especially when confronted with extraordinary and outrageous intrusions into my analytic space—was vital for the patient's development and eventual well-being. I believe that my survival helped the patient achieve a victory over the forces of Thanatos.

2. *Holding relationship*. Providing the patient with a nurturing, confiding, and reflecting relationship, which included faith in his capabilities to grow as a result of the treatment, enabled him to feel some security in analysis and subsequently in life. This holding relationship facilitated the strengthening of the patient's psychic forces and the stabilization of his psychic boundaries.

3. *Hope*. Hope, which was clearly lacking in this patient, is the activation of an internalized relationship with a good object—a benign, reflective presence that makes thinking about the vicissitudes of emotional life possible, however frightening, disturbing, or unacceptable emotional responses might feel. Hope grows from

the repeated experience of being able to overcome or to manage painful states of mind in oneself whether triggered by the actions of others towards the self or by the actions of the self through aggressive acts (Lemma, 2004).

Hope is different from manic repression of feelings of loss and despair in that it is grounded in an acknowledgement of loss. It denotes a state of mind that allows the individual to approach externally and internally difficult scenarios with a sense that the difficulty can probably be overcome, even if this is painful and the process involves relinquishing past hopes. Lemma regards hope as "a profoundly moving and sobering appreciation of 'the possible', or of reality, reminiscent of Kierkegaard's (2000) definition of hope as 'passion for the possible'" (Lemma, 2004, p. 109).

Elie Wiesel (1977) makes reference to hope with regard to the Holocaust: "How do you unveil horrors without offering at the same time some measure of hope?" (p. 6). One of my psychoanalytic goals was to bring some hope into this treatment, particularly because the patient had to deal with the horrors of the present superimposed on those of the past. I attempted to achieve this goal through my interpretations, which, in addition to conveying an understanding of the patient's deepest anxieties, were intended to provide a kind of "mutative support" (De Jonghe, Rijnierse, & Janssen, 1992). Through interpretation, but also by my presence, I became a new kind of introject (Pollock, 1964), which, in contrast to the earlier one, provided hope.

In my view, it is Eros, the life-force, that is conveyed through the analyst's stance and that often stems the tide of Thanatos, the death-force. That is not to say that Thanatos completely disappears from one's life, but that it becomes tamed by the life-force and comes under its control. In this connection, I want to quote Betty Joseph's (1982) eloquent words:

> I have described the pull of death instincts, the pull towards near-death, a kind of mental or physical brinkmanship in which the seeing of the self in this dilemma, unable to be helped, is an essential aspect. It is however important to consider where the pull towards life and sanity is. I believe that this part of the patient is located in the analyst. [p. 128]

I believe that, in this case, the pull towards life and sanity that my patient located in me, as well as my own fight against Thanatos, and my own faith in psychoanalysis as an instrument for development and growth, were crucial aspects of this treatment.

REFERENCES

Akhtar, S. (1992). *Broken Structures: Severe Personality Disorders and Their Treatment*. Northvale, NJ: Jason Aronson.

Akhtar, S. (1998). Psychoanalysis and the rainbow of cultural authenticity. In: S. Akhtar & S. Kramer (Eds.), *Colors of Childhood: Separation–Individuation Across Cultural, Racial, and Ethnic Differences* (pp. 113–129). Northvale, NJ/London: Jason Aronson.

Akhtar, S. (1999). Psychoanalysis and psychodynamic psychotherapy. In: *Immigration and Identity: Turmoil, Treatment and Transformation* (pp. 109–139). Northvale, NJ/London: Jason Aronson.

Akhtar, S. (2000). Mental pain and the cultural ointment of poetry. *International Journal of Psychoanalysis, 81*: 229–245.

Akhtar, S. (2001). From mental pain to manic defense to mourning. In: S. Akhtar (Ed.), *Three Faces of Mourning: Melancholia, Manic Defense and Moving On* (pp. 95–115). North Bergen, NJ: Jason Aronson.

Akhtar, S. (Ed.) (2006). *Interpersonal Boundaries: Variations and Violations*. New York: Jason Aronson.

Anzieu, D. (1985). *Le moi-peau*. Paris: Dunod.

Anzieu, D. (1989). *The Skin Ego*, trans. C. Turner. New Haven, CT/London: Yale University Press.

Apprey, M. (1991). Psychical transformations by a child of incest. In: S. Kramer & S. Akhtar (Eds.), *The Trauma of Transgression* (pp. 115–148). Northvale, NJ: Jason Aronson.

Auerhahn, N. C., & Laub, D. (1998). Intergenerational memory of the Holocaust. In: Y. Danieli (Ed.), *International Handbook of Multigenerational Legacies of Trauma* (pp. 21–43). New York/London: Plenum Press.

Auerhahn, N. C., & Prelinger, E. (1983). Repetition in the concentration camp survivor and her child. *International Review of Psychoanalysis, 10*: 31–46.

Axelrod, S., Schnipper, O. L., & Rau, J. H. (1978). "Hospitalized Offspring of Holocaust Survivors: Problems and Dynamics." Paper presented at the Annual Meeting of the American Psychiatric Association (May).

Barocas, H. A., & Barocas, C. B. (1973). Manifestations of concentration camp effects on the second generation. *American Journal of Psychiatry, 130*: 8201.

Becker, C. L. (1955). What are historical facts? *Western Political Quarterly, 8* (3).

Benedek, T. (1956). Toward the biology of the depressive constellation. *Journal of American Psychoanalytic Association, 4*: 389–427.

Bergmann, M. S., & Jucovy, M. E. (Eds.) (1982). *Generations of the Holocaust.* New York: Basic Books.

Bick, E. (1968). The experience of the skin in early object relations. *International Journal of Psychoanalysis, 49*: 484–486.

Blum, H. P. (1973). The concept of eroticized transference. *Journal of the American Psychoanalytic Association, 21*: 61–76.

Blum, H. P. (1985). Superego formation, adolescent transformation, and the adult neurosis. *Journal of the American Psychoanalytic Association, 33*: 887–909.

Blum, H. P. (1996). Seduction trauma and pathogenesis. *Journal of the American Psychoanalytic Association, 44*: 1147–1164.

Bowlby, J. (1961). Processes of mourning. *International Journal of Psychoanalysis, 42*: 317–340.

Bowlby, J. (1973). *Attachment and Loss, Vol. 2: Separation: Anxiety and Anger.* New York: Basic Books.

Brenner, I. (2002). Foreword. In: V. D. Volkan, G. Ast, & W. F. Greer, Jr., *The Third Reich in the Unconscious: Transgenerational Transmission and Its Consequences* (pp. xi–xvii). New York/London: Brunner-Routledge.

Brenner, I. (2004). *Psychic Trauma: Dynamics, Symptoms and Treatment.* Lanham, BO/New York/Toronto/Oxford: Jason Aronson.

Burch, B. (1989). Mourning and failure to mourn: An object-relations view. *Contemporary Psychoanalysis. 25*: 608–623.

Burlingham, D. T., Goldberger, A., & Lussier, A. (1955). Simultaneous analysis of mother and child. *Psychoanalytic Study of the Child, 10*: 165–186.

Chasseguet-Smirgel, J. (1978). Reflections on the connections between sadism and perversion. *International Journal of Psychoanalysis, 59*: 27–35.

Chasseguet-Smirgel, J. (1984). *Creativity and Perversion.* New York: Norton.

Chasseguet-Smirgel, J. (1996). The archaic matrix of the Oedipus complex. In *Sexuality and Mind: The Role of the Father and the Mother in the Psyche* (pp. 74–92). New York/London: New York University Press.

Cohen, Y. (2006). "The Experience of Oneness: Its Essential Role in the Development of Selfhood." Paper presented at the Fifth Conference of the Child and Adolescent Section of the EFPP.

Colby, K. M. (1949). Human symbiosis. *Psychiatry, 12.*

De Jonghe, F., Rijnierse, P., & Janssen, R. (1992). The role of support in psychoanalysis. *Journal of the American Psychoanalytic Association, 40*: 475–499.

Denett, D. (1987). *The Intentional Stance.* Cambridge, MA: MIT Press.

Dorpat, T. L. (1979). Is splitting a defense? *International Review of Psychoanalysis, 6*: 105–113.

Dorpat, T. L. (1987). A new look at denial and defense. *Annual of Psychoanalysis, 15*: 23–47.

Epstein, M. (1990). Beyond the oceanic feeling: Psychoanalytic study of Buddhist meditation. *International Review of Psychoanalysis, 17*: 159–164.

Epstein, R. S. (1994). *Keeping Boundaries: Maintaining Safety and Integrity in the Psychotherapeutic Process.* Washington, DC: American Psychiatric Press.

Erikson, E. H. (1956). The problem of ego identity. *Journal of the American Psychoanalytic Association, 4*: 56–121. Also in: *Identity and the Life Cycle* (pp. 104–64). New York: International Universities Press, 1959.

Erlich, S. (1978). Adolescent suicide: Maternal longing and cognitive development. *Psychoanalytic Study of the Child, 33*: 261–277.

Erlich, S. (1990). Boundaries, limitations, and the wish for fusion in the treatment of adolescents. *Psychoanalytic Study of the Child, 45*: 195–213.

Etchegoyen, R. H. (1977). Perversion of transference: Theoretical and technical aspects. In: L. Grinberg (ed.), *Practicos psicoanaliticas comparados en las psicosis* (pp. 58–83). Buenos Aires: Paidos.

Evelyn-White, H. G. (Trans.) (1914). *The Theogony.* In: *Hesiod: The Homeric Hymns and Homerica.* Loeb Classical Library. Cambridge, MA: Harvard University Press, 1964.

Federn, P. (1952). The ego as a subject and object in narcissism. In: E. Weiss (Ed.) *Ego Psychology and the Psychoses* (pp. 283–322). New York: Basic Books.

Fingarette, H. (1969). *Self-Deception.* New York: Routledge & Kegan Paul.

Fischer, R. M. S. (1991). The unresolved rapprochement crisis: An important constituent of the incest experience. In: S. Kramer & S. Akhtar (Eds.), *The Trauma of Transgression* (pp. 39–56). Northvale, NJ: Jason Aronson.

Fonagy, P., Steele, M., Steele, H., Moran, G., & Higgitt, A. C. (1991). The capacity for understanding mental states: The reflective self in parent and child and its significance for security of attachment. *Infant Mental Health Journal, 13*: 200–217.

Fresco, N. (1984). Remembering the unknown. *International Review of Psychoanalysis, 11*: 417–427

Freud, A. (1936). *The Ego and the Mechanisms of Defense.* New York: International Universities Press, 1966.

Freud, A. (1958). Adolescence. *Psychoanalytic Study of the Child, 13*: 255–278

Freud, A. (1960). Discussion of Dr. John Bowlby's paper. *Psychoanalytic Study of the Child, 15*: 53–62.

Freud, A. (1967). Comments on trauma. In: S. Furst (Ed.), *Psychic Trauma.* New York: Basic Books.

Freud, A. (1969). Adolescence as a developmental disturbance. *Writings, 7*: 39–47.

Freud, A., & Burlingham, D. (1944). *Infants without Families.* New York: International Universities Press.

Freud, S. (1911b). Formulations on the two principles of mental functioning. *Standard Edition, 12*: 213–37.

Freud, S. (1912–13). *Totem and Taboo. Standard Edition, 13*: 1–162.

Freud, S. (1915e). The unconscious. *Standard Edition, 14*: 159–237.

Freud, S. (1917e [1915]). Mourning and melancholia. *Standard Edition, 14*: 237–259.

Freud, S. (1920g). *Beyond the Pleasure Principle. Standard Edition, 18*: 7–64.

Freud, S. (1923e). The infantile genital organization. *Standard Edition, 19*: 141–149.

Freud, S. (1926d [1925]). *Inhibitions, Symptoms and Anxiety. Standard Edition, 20*: 75–175

Freud, S. (1930a). *Civilization and Its Discontents. Standard Edition, 21*: 64–149.

Freud, S. (1939a [1937–39]). *Moses and Monotheism. Standard Edition, 23*: 1–139.

Freud, S. (1940e [1938]). Splitting of the ego in the processes of defence. *Standard Edition, 23*: 271–279.

Freud, S. (1950 [1895]). Project for a scientific psychology. *Standard Edition, 1*: 281–388.

Freyberg, S. (1980). Difficulties in separation–individuation, as experienced by offspring of Nazi Holocaust survivors. *American Journal of Orthopsychiatry, 5*: 87–95.

Gabbard, G. O., & Lester, E. P. (1995). *Boundaries and Boundary Violations in Psychoanalysis.* Washington, DC/London: American Psychiatric Publishing.

Gaddini, E. (1972). Beyond the death instinct: Problems of psychoanalytic research on aggression. In: A. Limentani (Ed.), *A Psychoanalytic Theory of Infantile Experience: Conceptual and Clinical Reflections*. London: Routledge.

Gampel, Y. (1982). A daughter of silence. In: M. S. Bergmann & M. E. Jucovy (Eds.), *Generations of the Holocaust* (pp. 120–136). New York: Basic Books.

Gampel, Y. (1986). *L'effrayant et le menaçant. De la transmission à la répétition.* Psychanalyse à l'Université, *11* (41): 87–102.

Gampel, Y. (2005). *Ces parents qui vivent à travers moi. Les enfants des guerres.* Paris: Fayard.

Garland, C. B. (1991). External disasters and the internal world: An approach to psychotherapeutic understanding of survivors. In: J. Holmes (Ed.), *Textbook of Psychotherapy in Psychiatric Practice*. London: Churchill Livingstone.

Garland, C. B. (Ed.) (2002). *Understanding Trauma: A Psychoanalytical Approach* (2nd enlarged edition). London: Karnac.

Glover, E. (1956). Development of the body ego. *Psychoanalytic Study of the Child, 5*: 19–23.

Grand, S. (2000). *The Reproduction of Evil: A Clinical and Cultural Perspective.* Hillsdale, NJ: Analytic Press.

Green, A. (1986). The dead mother. In: *On Private Madness* (pp. 142–174). London: Hogarth Press.

Greenacre, P. (1967). The influence of infantile trauma on genetic patterns. In: S. S. Furst (Ed.), *Psychic Trauma* (pp. 260–299). New York/London: Basic Books.

Grinberg, L. (1964). Two kinds of guilt: Their relations with normal and pathological aspects of mourning. *International Journal of Psychoanalysis, 45*: 366–371.

Grinberg, L. (1992). Persecutory guilt. In: *Guilt and Depression* (pp. 80–87). London: Karnac.

Grinberg, L., & Grinberg, R. (1974). The problem of identity and the psychoanalytical process. *International Journal of Psychoanalysis, 1*: 499–507.

Grubrich-Simitis, I. (1984). From concretism to metaphor. *Psychoanalytic Study of the Child, 39*: 301–319.

Halberstadt-Freud, H. C. (1989). Electra in bondage: On symbiosis and the symbiotic illusion between mother and daughter and the consequences for the Oedipus complex. *Free Associations, 17*: 58–89.

Halberstadt-Freud, H. C. (1991). *Freud, Proust, Perversion and Love.* Amsterdam/Lisse: Swets & Zeitlinger.

Harrison, I. B. (1979). On Freud's view of the infant–mother relationship and of the oceanic feeling: Some subjective influences. *Journal of the American Psychoanalytic Association, 27*: 399–421.

Hartmann, H. (1964). *Essays on Ego Psychology*. New York: International Universities Press.

Hartmann, H. (1991). *Boundaries in the Mind: A New Psychology of Personality*. New York: Basic Books.

Hilgard, E. R. (1949). Human motives and the concept of the self. *American Psychologist, 4*: 374–382.

Hoffer, W. (1950). Development of the body ego. *Psychoanalytic Study of the Child, 5*: 19–23.

Houzel, D. (1987). The concept of psychic envelope. In: D. Anzieu (Ed.), *Psychic Envelopes* (pp. 27–59). London: Karnac, 1990.

Inhelder, B., & Piaget, J. (1958). *The Growth of Logical Thinking from Childhood to Adolescence*. New York: Basic Books.

Jacobson, E. (1959). Denial and repression. *Journal of the American Psychoanalytic Association, 7*: 581–609.

Jacobson, E. (1964). *The Self and the Object World*. New York: International Universities Press.

Joffe, W. G., & Sandler, J. (1965). Pain, depression and individuation. In: J. Sandler (Ed.), *From Safety to Superego*. New York: Guilford Press; London: Karnac, 1987.

Jones, E. (1957). *Sigmund Freud: Life and Work, Vol. 3*. London: Hogarth Press.

Joseph, B. (1982). Addiction to near-death. In: M. Feldman & E. Bott Spillius (Eds.), *Psychic Equilibrium and Psychic Change* (pp. 127–139). London/New York: Tavistock, Routledge, 1991.

Kernberg, O. F. (1995). Foreword. In: *Boundaries and Boundary Violations*. Washington, DC/London: American Psychiatric Publishing.

Kestenberg, J. S. (1972). How children remember and parents forget. *International Journal of Psychoanalytic Psychotherapy, 1–2*: 103–123.

Kestenberg, J. S. (1980). Psychoanalyses of children of survivors from the Holocaust: Case presentations and assessment. *Journal of American Psychoanalytic Association, 28*: 775–804.

Kestenberg, J. S., & Brenner, I. (1996). *The Last Witness*. Washington, DC: American Psychiatric Press.

Khan, M. M. R. (1962). The role of polymorph-perverse body experiences and object relations in ego integration. In: *Alienation in Perversions* (pp. 31–56). London: Hogarth Press, 1979.

Khan, M. M. R. (1974). La rancune de l'hystérique. *Nouvelle Revue de Psychanalyse, 10*: 151–158.

Khan, M. M. R. (1979). *Alienation in Perversions*. London: Hogarth Press.

Kierkegaard, S. (2000). *The Living Thoughts of Kierkegaard*, ed. W. H. Auden. New York: The New York Review of Books.

Klein, G. (1959). Consciousness in psychoanalytic theory: Some implications for current research in perception. *Journal of the American Psychoanalytic Association*, 7: 5–34.

Klein, H. (1971). Families of Holocaust survivors in the kibbutz: Psychological studies. In: H. Krystal & W. Niederland (Eds.), *Psychic Traumatisation: After-Effects in Individuals and Communities*. Boston, MA: Little & Brown.

Klein, H. (1981). Yale Symposium on the Holocaust. *Proceedings* (September).

Klein, H., & Kogan, I. (1986). Identification and denial in the shadow of Nazism. *International Journal of Psychoanalysis*, 67: 45–52. Also in: S. Brose & G. Pagel (Eds.), *Psychoanalyse im Exil. Texte Verfolgter Analytiker* (pp. 128–137). Würzburg: Königshausen & Neumann, 1987.

Klein, M. (1935). A contribution to the psychogenesis of manic-depressive states. In: *Love, Guilt and Reparation, and Other Works, 1921–1945* (pp. 262–289). New York: Free Press, 1975.

Kogan, I. (1989). Working through the vicissitudes of trauma in the psychoanalyses of Holocaust survivors' offspring. *Sigmund Freud House Bulletin*, 13 (2): 25-35. Also in: *Psyche, Zeitschrift für Psychoanalyse und ihre Anwendungen*, 6 (1990): 533–545.

Kogan, I. (1990). A journey to pain. *International Journal of Psychoanalysis*, 1: 629–640.

Kogan, I. (1995). *The Cry of Mute Children—A Psychoanalytic Perspective of the Second Generation of the Holocaust*. London/New York: Free Association Books.

Kogan, I. (1998). The black hole of dread: The psychic reality of children of Holocaust survivors. In: J. H. Berke, S. Pierides, A. Sobbaddini, & S. Schneider (Eds.), *Even Paranoids Have Enemies: New Perspectives on Paranoia and Persecution* (pp. 47–59). London & New York: Routledge.

Kogan, I. (2002). "Enactment" in the lives and treatment of Holocaust survivors' offspring. *Psychoanalytic Quarterly*, 71 (2): 251–273.

Kogan, I. (2003). On being a dead, beloved child. *Psychoanalytic Quarterly*, 72 (3): 727–767.

Kogan, I. (2004). "Working with Holocaust Survivors' Offspring in the Shadow of Terror." Paper presented at the IPA Congress, New Orleans, on the Panel: Working with Psychotic and Non-Psychotic Patients in Situations of Terror and Military Dictatorships.

Kramer, S. (1983). Object-coercive doubting: A pathological defense response to maternal incest. *Journal of the American Psychoanalytic Association*, 31: 325–351.

Kramer, S. (1991). Psychopathological effects of incest. In: S. Kramer & S. Akhtar (Eds.), *The Trauma of Transgression* (pp. 1–12). Northvale, NJ: Jason Aronson.

Kramer, S. (1994). Further considerations of somatic and cognitive residues of incest. In: A. Sugarman (Ed.), *Victims of Abuse* (pp. 69–96). Madison, CT: International Universities Press.

Krapf, E. E. (1956). Cold and warmth in the transference experience. *International Journal of Psychoanalysis, 37*: 389–391.

Krell, R. (1979). Holocaust families: The survivors and their children. *Comprehensive Psychiatry, 20* (6): 560–567.

Kris, E. (1956). The personal myth: A problem in psychoanalytic technique. *Journal of the American Psychoanalytic Association, 4*: 653–681.

Krystal, H. (1968). Some types of psychological damage not subsumed under concepts of mental trauma. In: H. Krystal (Ed.), *Massive Psychic Trauma* (pp. 2–8). New York: International Universities Press.

Kuchenhoff, J. (1998). The body and the ego boundaries: A case study on psychoanalytic therapy with psychosomatic patients. *Psychoanalytic Inquiry, 18*: 368–382.

Landis, B. (1970). Ego boundaries. *Psychological Issues Monograph, 4*: 1–177.

Laplanche, J., & Pontalis, J.-P. (1967). *The Language of Psychoanalysis*. New York: Norton, 1973.

Laub, D., & Auerhahn, N. C. (1984). Reverberations of genocide: Its expression in the conscious and unconscious of post-Holocaust generations. In: S. A. Luel & P. Marcus (Eds.), *Psychoanalytic Reflections of the Holocaust: Selected Essays* (pp. 151–167). Denver: Ktav Publishing.

Laub, D., & Auerhahn, N. C. (1993). Knowing and not knowing psychic trauma: Forms of traumatic memory. *International Journal of Psychoanalysis, 74*: 287–302.

Laufer, M. (1973). The analysis of a child of survivors. In: E. J. Anthony & C. Koupernik, (Eds.), *The Child in His Family: The Impact of Disease and Death, Vol. 2* (pp. 363–373). New York: John Wiley.

Lemma, A. (2004). On hope's tightrope: Reflections on the capacity for hope. In: S. Levy & A. Lemma (Eds.), *The Perversion of Loss*. London/Philadelphia: Whurr.

Lester, E. P. (1994). Review of *Boundaries in the Mind* by Ernest Hartmann (New York. Basic Books. 1991). *International Journal of Psychoanalysis, 81*: 229–245.

Lewin, B. (1950). *The Psychoanalysis of Elation*. New York: Norton.

Lifton, R. J. (1978). Witnessing survival. *Transactions* (March): 40–44.

Lipkowitz, M. H. (1973). The child of two survivors: The report of an unsuccessful therapy. *Israeli Annals of Psychiatry and Related Disciplines, 2* (2): 363–374.

Loftus, E. F., & Loftus, G. R. (1980). On the permanence of stored information in the human brain. *American Psychologist, 5*: 405–420.

Mahler, M. S. (1952). On childhood psychosis and schizophrenia: Autistic and symbiotic infantile psychosis. *Psychoanalytic Study of the Child, 7*: 286–305.

Mahler, M. S. (1961). On sadness and grief in infancy and childhood: Loss and restitution of the symbiotic love object. *Psychoanalytic Study of the Child, 16*: 322–351.

Mahler, M. S. (1968). *On Human Symbiosis and the Vicissitudes of Individuation, Vol. 1: Infantile Psychosis.* New York: International Universities Press.

Mahler, M. S. (1972). Rapprochement subphase of the separation–individuation process. *Psychoanalytic Quarterly, 41*: 487–506.

Mahler, M. S., Pine, F., & Bergmann, A. (1975). *The Psychological Birth of the Human Infant.* New York: Basic Books.

McDougall, J. (1989). *Theatres of the Body: A Psychoanalytic Approach to Somatic Illness.* London: Free Association Books.

McLaughlin, J. (1995). Touching limits in the analytic dyad. *Psychoanalytic Quarterly, 64*: 433–465.

Meissner, W. W. (1984). *Psychoanalysis and Religious Experience.* New Haven, CT: Yale University Press.

Metcalf, A. (1977). Childhood: From process to structure. In: M. J. Horowitz (Ed.), *Hysterical Personality* (pp. 223–281). New York: Jason Aronson.

Micheels, L. J. (1985). Bearer of the secret. *Psychoanalytic Inquiry, 5*: 21–30.

Milner, M. (1952). Aspects of symbolism in comprehension of the not-self. *International Journal of Psychoanalysis, 33*: 181–194.

Milner, M. (1969). *The Hands of the Living God.* London: Virago Press, 1988.

Modell, A. H. (1961). Denial and the sense of separateness. *Journal of the American Psychoanalytic Association, 9*: 533–547.

Moses, R. (Ed.) (1993). *Persistent Shadows of the Holocaust: The Meaning to Those Not Directly Affected.* Madison, CT: International Universities Press.

Ogden, T. H. (1966). The perverse subject of analysis. *Journal of the American Psychoanalytic Association, 44*: 1121–1146.

Ogden, T. H. (1986). *The Matrix of the Mind.* New York: Jason Aronson.

Oliner, M. M. (1982). Hysterical features among children of survivors. In: M. S. Bergmann & M. E. Jucovy (Eds.), *Generations of the Holocaust* (pp. 267–285). New York: Basic Books..

Person, E. S. (1988). Review of *Creativity and Perversion*: Janine Chasseguet-Smirgel (New York: Norton, 1984). *Journal of the American Psychoanalytic Association, 36*: 1067–1071.

Phillips, R. (1978). Impact of Nazi Holocaust on children of survivors. *American Journal of Psychotherapy, 32*: 370–377.

Pines, D. (1980). Skin communication: Early skin disorders and their effect on transference and countertransference. *International Journal of Psychoanalysis, 61*: 315–322. Also in: *A Woman's Unconscious Use of Her Body: A Psychoanalytical Perspective* (pp. 8–26). London: Virago, 1993.

Pollock, G. H. (1961). Mourning and adaptation. *International Journal of Psychoanalysis, 42*: 341–361.

Pollock, G. H. (1964). On symbiosis and symbiotic neurosis. *International Journal of Psychoanalysis, 45*: 1–30.

Pollock, G. H. (1978). Process and affect: Mourning and grief. *International Journal of Psychoanalysis, 59*: 255–276.

Pontalis, J. B. (1981). *Frontiers in Psychoanalysis: Between the Dream and Psychic Reality*. New York: International Universities Press.

Racamier, P. C. (1952). Hystérie et théâtre. In: *De psychanalyse en psychiatrie* (pp. 135–164). Paris: Payot, 1979.

Rachman, A. W. (1989). Confusion of tongues: The Ferenczian metaphor for childhood seduction and emotional trauma. *Journal of the American Academy of Psychoanalysis, 17*: 182–205.

Rachman, A. W. (1997). The suppression and censorship of Ferenczi's "Confusion of Tongues" paper. *Psychoanalytic Inquiry, 17*: 182–205.

Rakoff, V. (1966). Long-term effects of the concentration camp experience. *Viewpoints, 1*: 17–21.

Roland, A. (1988). *In Search of Self in India and Japan: Toward a Cross-Cultural Psychology*. Princeton, NJ: Princeton University Press.

Rosenfeld, H. A. (1983). Primitive object relations and mechanisms. *International Journal of Psychoanalysis, 64*: 261–267.

Rosenfeld, H. A. (1987). *Impasse and Interpretation*. London/New York: Tavistock.

Roth, S. (1993). The shadow of the Holocaust. In: R. Moses (Ed.), *Persistent Shadows of the Holocaust: The Meaning to Those Not Directly Affected* (pp. 37–79). Madison, CT: International Universities Press.

Sandler, J. (1983). Reflections on some relations between psychoanalytic concepts and psychoanalytic practice. *International Journal of Psychoanalysis, 64*: 35–45.

Schaeffer, S. F. (1980). The unreality of realism. *Critical Inquiry, 6*: 727–738.

Schafer, R. (1968). The mechanisms of defense. *International Journal of Psychoanalysis, 49*: 49–62.

Schafer, R. (1976). *A New Language for Psychoanalysis*. New Haven/London: Yale University Press.

Schneider, S., & Berke, J. H. (in press). The oceanic feelings, mysticism and Kabbalah: Freud's historical roots. *Psychoanalytic Review*.

Segal, H. (1983). Some clinical implications of Melanie Klein's work. *International Journal of Psychoanalysis, 64*: 269–276.

Sonnenberg, S. M. (1974). Children of survivors: Workshop report. *Journal of the American Psychoanalytic Association, 22*: 200–204.

Steele, B. E. (1991). The psychopathology of incest participants. In: S. Kramer & S. Akhtar (Eds.), *The Trauma of Transgression* (pp. 13–38). Northvale, NJ: Jason Aronson.

Steiner, J. (1993). *Psychic Retreats: Pathological Organizations in Psychotic, Neurotic and Borderline Patients*. New York: Brunner-Routledge.

Stevens, W. (1954). Esthétique du mal. In: *Collected Poems* (pp. 313–325). New York: Alfred A. Knopf. Reprinted New York: Vintage Books, 1990. Republished New York: Library of America, 1997.

Stoller, R. (1975). *Perversion.* New York: Pantheon.

Trossman, B. (1968). Adolescent children of concentration camp survivors. *Canadian Psychiatric Association Journal, 12*: 121–123.

Turner, F. J. (1938). The significance of history. In: *The Early Writings of Frederick Jackson Turner.* Madison, WI: University of Wisconsin Press.

Volkan, V. D., Ast, G., & Greer, W. F. (2002). *The Third Reich in the Unconscious.* New York/London: Brunner-Routledge.

Waelder, R. (1951). The structure of paranoid ideas. *International Journal of Psychoanalysis, 32*: 167–177.

Weisman, A. D. (1972). *On Dying and Denying. A Psychiatric Study of Terminality.* New York: Behavioral Publications.

Weiss, E. (1934). Bodily pain and mental pain. *International Journal of Psychoanalysis, 15*: 1–13.

Welldon, E. V. (1993). *Madre, virgen, puta. Idealización y denigración de la maternidad* [Mother, madonna, whore: The idealization and denigration of motherhood]. Madrid: Siglo XXI.

Werman, D. S. (1986). On the nature of the oceanic experience. *Journal of the American Psychoanalytic Association, 34*: 123–139.

Wiesel, E. (1977). The Holocaust: Three views. *ADL Bulletin* (November).

Winnicott, D. W. (1935). The manic defence. In: *Collected Papers: Through Paediatrics to Psychoanalysis* (pp. 129–144). London: Tavistock.

Winnicott, D. W. (1962). Ego integration in child development. In: *The Maturational Processes and the Facilitating Environment* (pp. 56–64). London: Hogarth Press, 1965.

Winnicott, D. W. (1967). Mirror-role of the mother and family in child development. In: P. Lomas (Ed.), *The Predicament of the Family: A Psychoanalytic Symposium* (pp. 26–33). London: Hogarth Press. Reprinted in: D. W. Winnicott, *Playing and Reality* (pp. 111–118). London: Tavistock, 1971.

Winnicott, D. W. (1971). The use of an object and relating through identification. In: *Playing and Reality* (pp. 101–112). London: Tavistock.

INDEX